SHARE
the
Music

McGRAW-HILL

AUTHORS

Judy Bond,
Coordinating Author
René Boyer-White
Margaret Campbelle-duGard
Marilyn Copeland Davidson,
Coordinating Author
Robert de Frece
Mary Goetze,
Coordinating Author
Doug Goodkin
Betsy M. Henderson

Michael Jothen
Carol King
Vincent P. Lawrence,
Coordinating Author
Nancy L. T. Miller
Ivy Rawlins
Susan Snyder,
Coordinating Author

Janet McMillion,
Contributing Writer

McGraw-Hill
School Division

New York   Farmington

ACKNOWLEDGMENTS

Grateful acknowledgment is given to the following authors, composers, and publishers. Every effort has been made to trace the ownership of all copyrighted material and to secure the necessary permissions to reprint these selections. In the case of some selections for which acknowledgment is not given, extensive research has failed to locate the copyright holders.

American Folklore Society for *Stone Pounding*, edited by T. Grame. Reprinted by permission of the American Folklore Society.

Argus Magazine for *I wonder how it feels to fly* by Earl Thompson. Courtesy of Argus Magazine, Seattle, WA.

Association for Childhood Education International for *I Wish* (aka *The Shiny Little House*) from SUNG UNDER THE SILVER UMBRELLA by Nancy M. Hayes. Reprinted by permission of the Association for Childhood Education International, 11141 Georgia Avenue, Suite 200, Wheaton, MD 20902. Copyright © 1935 by the Association.

Elizabeth Barnett for *Counting-out Rhyme* by Edna St. Vincent Millay. From COLLECTED POEMS, Harper & Row. Copyright © 1928, 1955 by Edna St. Vincent Millay and Norma Millay Ellis. Reprinted by permission of Elizabeth Barnett, literary executor.

Board of Jewish Education of Greater New York for *Hashkëdiya (The Almond Tree)* by M. Ravina, Y. Dushman, and S. Dinin from THE NEW JEWISH SONG BOOK by Harry Coopersmith, © 1965 Harry Coopersmith, published by Board of Jewish Education of Greater New York.

Boosey & Hawkes, Inc. for *The Derby Ram* by Peter Erdei from 150 AMERICAN FOLK SONGS. Copyright © 1974 by Boosey & Hawkes, Inc. Reprinted by permission. For *Dormi, Dormi,* arranged by Mary Goetze. Copyright © 1984 by Boosey & Hawkes, Inc. This arrangement is made with the permission of Boosey & Hawkes, Inc. Reprinted by permission. For *A Tragic Story* from FRIDAY AFTERNOONS by Benjamin Britten. © 1936 by Boosey & Co., Ltd.; Copyright renewed. Reprinted by permission of Boosey & Hawkes, Inc. For *Troika* from LIEUTENANT KIJE by S. Prokofiev. © 1936 by Edition A. Guthiel. Copyright assigned to Boosey & Hawkes, Inc.; Copyright Renewed. Reprinted by permission.

Marie Brown Associates for *Nathaniel's Rap* by Eloise Greenfield. Reprinted by permission of MARIE BROWN ASSOCIATES; © 1988 by Eloise Greenfield.

Canadian Museum of Civilization for *Feller from Fortune (Lots of Fish in Bonavist' Harbour)* from SONGS ON THE NEWFOUNDLAND OUTPORTS by Kenneth Peacock. National Museum of Canada, Bulletin 197, Anthropological Series 65, vol. 1, Ottawa 1965.

Cherry Lane Music Publishing Company, Inc. for *Calypso* by John Denver. © 1975 Cherry Lane Music Publishing Company, Inc. This Arrangement © 1994 Cherry Lane Music Publishing Company, Inc. All Rights Reserved. Used By Permission. For *Garden Song* by David Mallet. © Copyright 1975 Cherry Lane Music Publishing Company, Inc. This Arrangement © Copyright 1994 Cherry Lane Music Publishing Company, Inc. For *Grandma's Feather Bed* by Jim Connor. Copyright © 1973 Cherry River Music Company. International Copyright Secured. All Rights Reserved.

Choristers Guild for *Come and Sing Together* from CANONS, SONGS AND BLESSINGS by Helen and John Kemp. Copyright © 1990 Choristers Guild. Used by permission.

Vernon Clark for *Martin's Cry* by Vernon Clark. © 1991 Vernon Clark.

CPP/Belwin, Inc. for *Donna Donna* by Sholom Secunda and Aaron Zeitlin. Copyright © 1940, 1950 (Renewed 1968) MILLS MUSIC INC., c/o EMI MUSIC PUBLISHING. World Print Rights Administered by CPP/BELWIN, INC. All Rights Reserved. For *Petrushka* by Igor Stravinsky. Copyright © E.M. KALMUS ORCHESTRA SCORES. Used by Permission of CPP/Belwin, Inc., Miami, FL. All Rights Reserved. For *Singin' in the Rain* by Nacio Herb Brown & Arthur Freed. Copyright © 1929 (Renewed 1957) METRO-GOLDWYN-MAYER, INC., Rights Assigned to ROBBINS MUSIC CORP. All Rights of ROBBINS MUSIC CORP. Assigned to EMI CATALOGUE PARTNERSHIP. All Rights Controlled and Administered by EMI ROBBINS CATALOG, INC. International Copyright Secured. Made in U.S.A. Used by Permission. For *Sir Duke* by Stevie Wonder. © 1976 by JOBETE MUSIC CO., INC., and BLACKBULL MUSIC, INC., Hollywood, CA. International Copyright Secured. Made in USA. All Rights Reserved.

Dover Publications Inc. for *The California Song* from SONGS THE WHALEMEN SANG by Gale Huntington. © 1970 Dover Publications Inc.

continued on page 390

SPECIAL CONTRIBUTORS

Contributing Writer
Janet McMillion

Consultant Writers
Teri Burdette, Signing
Brian Burnett, Movement
Robert Duke, Assessment
Joan Gregoryk, Vocal Development/
  Choral
Judith Jellison, Special Learners/
  Assessment
Jacque Schrader, Movement
Kathy B. Sorensen, International Phonetic
  Alphabet
Mollie Tower, Listening

Consultants
Lisa DeLorenzo, Critical Thinking
Nancy Ferguson, Jazz/Improvisation
Judith Nayer, Poetry
Marta Sanchez, Dalcroze
Mollie Tower, Reviewer
Robyn Turner, Fine Arts

Multicultural Consultants
Judith Cook Tucker
JaFran Jones
Oscar Muñoz
Marta Sanchez
Edwin J. Schupman, Jr., of ORBIS
  Associates
Mary Shamrock
Kathy B. Sorensen

Multicultural Advisors
Shailaja Akkapeddi (Hindi), Edna Alba
(Ladino), Gregory Amobi (Ibu), Thomas
Appiah (Ga, Twi, Fanti), Deven Asay
(Russian), Vera Auman (Russian, Ukrainian),
David Azman (Hebrew), Lissa Bangeter
(Portuguese), Britt Marie Barnes (Swedish),
Dr. Mark Bell (French), Brad Ahawanrathe
Bonaparte (Mohawk), Chhanda Chakroborti
(Hindi), Ninthalangsonk Chanthasen
(Laotian), Julius Chavez (Navajo), Lin-Rong
Chen (Mandarin), Anna Cheng (Mandarin),
Rushen Chi (Mandarin), T. L. Chi (Mandarin),
Michelle Chingwa (Ottowa), Hoon Choi
(Korean), James Comarell (Greek), Lynn
DePaula (Portuguese), Ketan Dholakia
(Gujarati), Richard O. Effiong (Nigerian),
Nayereh Fallahi (Persian), Angela Fields
(Hopi, Chemehuevi), Gary Fields (Lakota,

Cree), Siri Veslemoy Fluge (Norwegian),
Katalin Forrai (Hungarian), Renee Galagos
(Swedish), Linda Goodman, Judith A. Gray,
Savyasachi Gupta (Marati), Elizabeth Haile
(Shinnecock), Mary Harouny (Persian),
Charlotte Heth (Cherokee), Tim Hunt
(Vietnamese), Marcela Janko (Czech), Raili
Jeffrey (Finnish), Rita Jensen (Danish), Teddy
Kaiahura (Swahili), Gueen Kalaw (Tagalog),
Merehau Kamai (Tahitian), Richard Keeling,
Masanori Kimura (Japanese), Chikahide
Komura (Japanese), Saul Korewa (Hebrew),
Jagadishwar Kota (Tamil), Sokun Koy
(Cambodian), Craig Kurumada (Balkan),
Cindy Trong Le (Vietnamese), Dongchoon Lee
(Korean), Young-Jing Lee (Korean), Nomi Lob
(Hebrew), Sam Loeng (Mandarin, Malay),
Georgia Magpie (Comanche), Mladen Marič
(Croatian), Kuinise Matagi (Samoan), Hiromi
Matsushita (Japanese), Jackie Maynard
(Hawaiian), David McAllester, Mike
Kanathohare McDonald (Mohawk),
Khumbulani Mdlefshe (Zulu), Martin Mkize
(Xhosa), David Montgomery (Turkish), Kazadi
Big Musungayi (Swahili), Professor Akiya
Nakamara (Japanese), Edwin Napia (Maori),
Hang Nguyen (Vietnamese), Richard Nielsen
(Danish), Wil Numkena (Hopi), Eva Ochoa
(Spanish), Drora Oren (Hebrew), Jackie
Osherow (Yiddish), Mavis Oswald (Russian),
Dr. Dil Parkinson (Arabic), Kenny Tahawisoren
Perkins (Mohawk), Alvin Petersen (Sotho),
Phay Phan (Cambodian), Charlie Phim
(Cambodian), Aroha Price (Maori), Marg Puiri
(Samoan), John Rainer (Taos Pueblo, Creek),
Lillian Rainer (Taos Pueblo, Creek, Apache),
Winton Ria (Maori), Arnold Richardson
(Haliwa-Saponi), Thea Roscher (German),
Dr. Wayne Sabey (Japanese), Regine Saintil
(Bamboula Creole), Luci Scherzer (German),
Ken Sekaquaptewa (Hopi), Samouen Seng
(Cambodian), Pei Shin (Mandarin), Dr. Larry
Shumway (Japanese), Gwen Shunatona
(Pawnee, Otoe, Potawatomi), Ernest Siva
(Cahuilla, Serrano [Maringa']), Ben Snowball
(Inuit), Dr. Michelle Stott (German), Keiko
Tanefuji (Japanese), James Taylor
(Portuguese), Shiu-wai Tong (Mandarin),
Tom Toronto (Lao, Thai), Lynn Tran
(Vietnamese), Gulavadee Vaz (Thai), Chen
Ying Wang (Taiwanese), Masakazu Watabe
(Japanese), Freddy Wheeler (Navajo), Keith
Yackeyonny (Comanche), Liming Yang
(Mandarin), Edgar Zurita (Andean)

CONTENTS

VOICES OF THE WORLD

There is music
in the hearts of people—
the music of joy
turned into song—
a roundelay of happiness—
lifting all voices
in one choir
of the world.

There is a dance-step
to the heart-beat of people—
a timing of gladness—
of nimble feet
and clapping hands—
widening around
the magic circle
of the world.

There is music
in the gypsy-tune
of violins—
a piper's flute—
the roll of an organ chord—
a tinkling chime—
the drum-beat
of a town-band on parade. . .
Music is the sound of life awakening
The voices of the world!

—*Stefi Samuelson*

WHERE IN THE WORLD?

1

A MUSICAL WORLD

Ella Fitzgerald

Louis Armstrong (Satchmo)

Duke Ellington

Is there anyone you look up to? Stevie Wonder expresses his admiration for some of his heroes in "Sir Duke."

Sir Duke

Words and Music by
Stevie Wonder

Verse

1. Mu - sic is a world with - in it - self
2. Mu - sic knows it is and al - ways will be

with a lan - guage we all un - der - stand,
one of the things that life just won't quit.

with an e - qual op - por - tu - ni - ty
But here are some of mu - sic's pi - o - neers,

for all to sing dance and clap their hands
that time will not al - low us to for - get

2

but just be-cause a re-cord has a groove don't make it in the groove
for there's— Ba-sie, Mil-ler, Satch-mo,— and the king of all, Sir Duke,

but you can tell right a-way at let-ter A— when the
and with a voice like— El-la's ring-in' out,— there's no

Refrain

peo-ple start to move. They} can feel it all— o - ver.—
way the band can lose. You}

They} can feel it all— o - ver,— peo-ple.— {They} can feel it all—
You}   {You}

o - ver.— {They} can feel it all— o - ver,— peo-ple, go!
         {You}

When you tap your foot to a song, you're tapping to the **beat,** or the steady pulse that you feel.

The long and short sounds and silences that occur when you sing the words are called the rhythm of the words.

CLAP the rhythm of the words in "Sir Duke." Then pat with the beat.

Count Basie

Glenn Miller

BOGGED DOWN BY BEATS?

Here's part of an Irish folk song, "Hi! Ho! The Rattlin' Bog."
Bogs are swampy areas where mosses float on top of plants.
A bog shakes or "rattles" when somebody steps on it.

Refrain

Hi! Ho! The rat-tlin' bog and the bog down in the val-ley-o.

Hi! Ho! The rat-tlin' bog and the bog down in the val-ley-o.

SING "Hi! Ho! The Rattlin' Bog," patting with the beats that feel stronger and clapping quietly with the other beats.

How are the strong and weak beats grouped?

The **meter signature** of a song shows how many beats are in each set. A song that has *one* strong and *one* weak beat in each set could have a meter signature with a 2 on the top.

Sets of beats can be felt differently. These patterns show beats that feel strong and weak.

Here's a folk song from the islands of Trinidad and Tobago.
As you listen, see if you can feel the beat.

I Let Her Go, Go

Folk Song from
Trinidad and Tobago
Adapted by Carol King

I let her go, go, Ee ay I let her go, go,

Ee ay I let her go ——— I let her go, go, go.

FIND the pattern on page 4 that shows
the set of beats used in this song. What
is the meter signature?

Musical Ideas Are Everywhere

Have you ever read a story without words? Try this one! Each picture stands for one idea. When all the ideas are put together, they tell a story.

Music is also made up of ideas. A complete musical idea is called a **phrase.** A phrase is made of high and low sounds, or **pitches.** When phrases are put together, they make up a song or a **melody.**

In a **call-and-response** song, call phrases are sung
by a leader and response phrases are sung by the group.
Find the phrases as you listen to this song.

'Way Down Yonder in the Brickyard

Traditional African
American Game Song
As Performed by the
Georgia Sea Island Singers

A Call **Freely**   Response

'Way down yon-der in the brick-yard,   Re-mem-ber me.

Call

'Way down yon-der in the brick-yard,   Re-mem-ber me.

B Call   Response

Oh, step it, step it,   step it down.____ Re-mem-ber me.

Call

Oh, step it, step it,   step it down.____ Re-mem-ber me.

C Call   Response

Oh, swing your la-dy,   turn her a-round,___ Re-mem-ber me.

Call

Oh, swing your la-dy,   turn her a-round,___ Re-mem-ber me.

A SONG FROM INNER MONGOLIA

Inner Mongolia is part of China. Some people live by herding animals, and the children help by watching over their families' sheep. The children may sing or play flutes to calm the flocks, just as you'd sing a lullaby to comfort a baby.

CHINESE MIRROR PAINTING
This mirror was painted when Qian-long was emperor of China (1735–1796). One woman plays a traditional flute, the other a frame drum and wooden clappers.

MOVE your arm in an arch to show each phrase you hear in "Mongolian Night Song." Then sing the song.

Traditional Inner Mongolian Song
Collected and Translated by Gloria Kiester

1. Lit - tle girl who tends the sheep, Brings them to the fold to sleep.
2. In the moon-light's gold - en glow, Soft the wind be - gins to blow.

Lit - tle lambs are bounc - ing by to their moth - er's bleat - ing cry,
Lit - tle lambs are fast a - sleep, ly - ing by the oth - er sheep.

Un-der-neath a star - lit sky.   All a - lone she waits.
Still a si - lent watch she keeps.

"In the dark I'm not a - fraid. I've a lamp to light the way."
"When I'm tend - ing all a - lone, All I think a - bout is home."

CHOICES WITH VOICES

Have you ever disguised your voice or tried to sound like somebody you know? Then you know you can change the sound of your speaking and singing voice.

LISTENING Mañana Iguana
by Bobby McFerrin

Bobby McFerrin uses his voice to make all sorts of interesting sounds. What are some things he does to change his voice?

One way to change your voice is to change the register. The **lighter register** is quieter and generally higher in pitch. The **heavier register** is usually louder, fuller, and lower in pitch.

SPEAK "I Wish" in the two registers.

I Wish

Nancy M. Hayes
Adapted by Carol King

1
I wish, how I wish, that I had a lit - tle house,

With a mat for the cat and a hole for the mouse,

And a clock go - ing "tock" in the cor - ner of the room

And a ket - tle, and a cup - board, and a big birch broom.

In a **canon,** all parts perform the same song or poem, but start at different times. Change the sound of the poem by speaking in canon. One group speaks in the heavier register, the other in the lighter register.

SING HIGH! SING LOW!

Using different registers, you change the **tone color** of your sound. You can sing different styles and make singing some pitches easier.

Compare two melodies. Most of the notes in "I Let Her Go, Go" are on the lower part of the staff. The lower pitches are probably easier to sing in the heavier register.

I   let   her   go, go,

Now look at the second melody. Are these notes mostly higher or lower than the ones in "I Let Her Go, Go"? Which register will you probably use to sing this part of "Hi! Ho! The Rattlin' Bog"?

Verse

Now   in this bog there was a tree, a   rare tree, a   rat-tlin' tree;

"Hi! Ho! The Rattlin' Bog" song is called a **cumulative** song because each verse adds to the story. Have a rattlin' good time!

Hi! Ho! The Rattlin' Bog

Irish
Folk Song

Refrain

Hi! Ho! The rat-tlin' bog and the bog down in the val-ley-o.

End here, last time

Hi! Ho! The rat-tlin' bog and the bog down in the val-ley-o.

Verse

1. Now in this bog there was a tree, a rare tree, a
2. Now on this tree there was a limb, a rare limb, a
3. Now on this limb there was a branch, a rare branch, a
4. Now on this branch there was a nest, a rare nest, a
5. Now in this nest there was an egg, a rare egg, a
6. Now in this egg there was a bird, a rare bird, a

Add a repeat with each verse

(Skip this measure for verse 1)

rat - tlin' tree; The
rat - tlin' limb; The limb on the tree and the
rat - tlin' branch; The branch on the limb and the
rat - tlin' nest; The nest on the branch and the
rat - tlin' egg; The egg in the nest and the
rat - tlin' bird; The bird in the egg and the

1.-6. tree in the bog and the bog down in the val - ley - o.

TIME OUT

Playing and resting are part of both sports and music.

Musical sounds have different lengths. Musicians know how long to play or sing by following written music. Look at the chart to see how musical sounds can be written when a quarter note gets the beat.

♩	**quarter note**	one sound to a beat
♫	two **eighth notes**	two sounds to a beat
♩	**half note**	sound lasting two beats
𝄽	**quarter rest**	silence the length of a beat

PAT each quarter note, snap the eighth notes, and brush your hands for each half note.

FOR RHYTHMS

THINK IT THROUGH

What are some movements you can make to show 𝄽 ?
Why did you choose those movements?

A **coda** is a special ending for a song or poem.

CREATE a coda for "I Wish" by performing the pattern on page 14 two times after you speak the poem.

STILL MUSIC

This painting shows a stage after a rehearsal or concert. Why do you think the artist, Ben Shahn, called it "Still Music"?

To see how sets of beats are felt in a song, look at the meter signature. The top number tells how many beats are in a set. The **bar lines** divide the notes into sets, or **measures,** based on the top number.

You can write $\frac{2}{\bullet}$ as $\frac{2}{4}$. The lower number tells what note lasts one beat. When there are three quarter notes in each measure, the meter signature can be written as $\frac{3}{4}$. What could you write if there were four quarter notes in each measure?

LISTEN for the sets of beats in "Mongolian Night Song." Decide where the missing bar lines go.

Lit - tle girl who tends the sheep

Brings them to the fold to sleep.

MELODIES TAKE SHAPE

Look at the shapes of three phrases from " 'Way Down Yonder in the Brickyard." The phrases use **pitch syllables** named *do re mi so*.

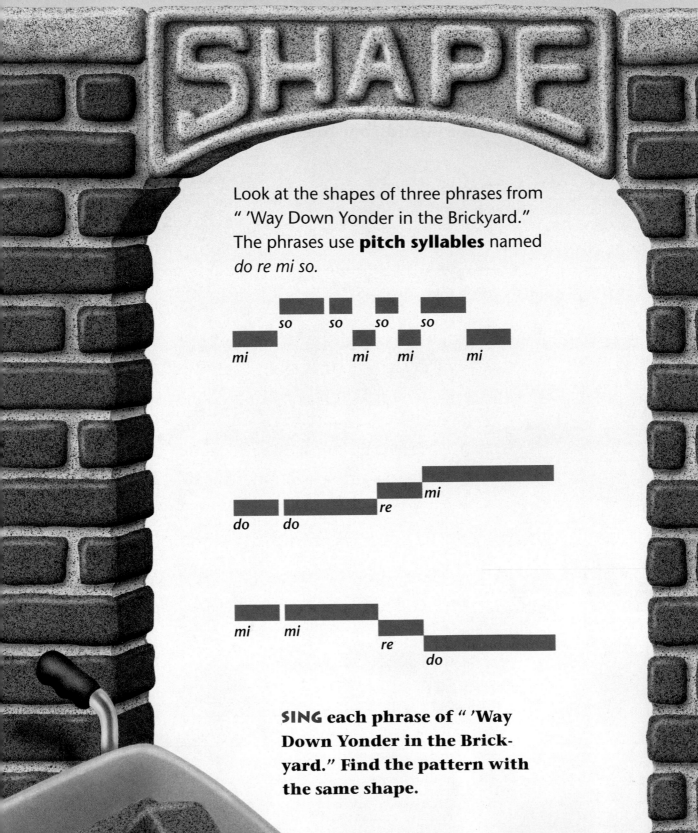

SING each phrase of " 'Way Down Yonder in the Brickyard." Find the pattern with the same shape.

Melodies can be written on a **staff** of five lines and four spaces. In " 'Way Down Yonder in the Brickyard," *do re mi so* look like this.

Because *do* is below the staff, an extra line called a **ledger line** is used.

MATCH these phrases with the patterns on page 18.

MOVING ON

You often hear *do* at the beginning and end of a song. *Do* can be written on any line or in any space of the staff. If *do* moves, the other pitches also move.

When *do* is on a line, where are *mi* and *so*? When *do* is in a space, where are *mi* and *so*?

LISTEN to some melodies. Which set of pitches do you hear?

People traditionally gathered to share folk songs, learning them from family and friends. Playing along on instruments, which were sometimes made at home, added to the fun.

Fed My Horse

Southern
Appalachian
Folk Song

Fed my horse in a pop-lar trough, Fed my horse in a pop-lar trough,

Fed my horse in a pop-lar trough, Then she caught the whoop-ing cough.

Coy ma-lin-do Kill-ko, kill-ko; Coy ma-lin-do Kill-ko me.

Which pitch sounded just right to end on?
Find the pitch in this song that is <u>not</u> *do re mi* or *so*.
The name of that pitch is *la*.

Just to Inform You

When you look at the shape or outline of something, you see its **form.** The form can be made up of one large shape or many smaller shapes.

DESCRIBE the forms in this building.

Music has form, too. You can hear the form of a song by listening to the order of its phrases or sections.

The order of a song's phrases is called its phrase form. To describe the form when two phrases are the same, use a a. When two phrases are different, use a b.

LISTEN to two phrases from a piece of music called "Troika."

Model of St. Basil's
Cathedral, Moscow

22

SPOTLIGHT ON
SERGEI PROKOFIEV

Sergei Prokofiev (1891–1953) was a renowned Russian pianist, conductor, and composer. His first piano teacher was his mother. He began composing when he was five, and tried to write an opera when he was nine. Prokofiev became a very good pianist, and once won a piano in a competition.

Prokofiev loved theater, and composed operas, ballets, and film music. He also wrote symphonies and concertos. Unusual stories attracted him. For example, he wrote music for Lieutenant Kijé, a movie about an imaginary man.

Prokofiev's music was criticized at first because people were not used to his modern harmonies and rhythms. However, others found his music brilliant and appealing, and he received many invitations to compose. Now he is remembered as one of the greatest modern composers.

LISTENING

Troika (excerpt) from *Lieutenant Kijé Suite*
by Sergei Prokofiev

Prokofiev wrote "Troika" as part of the music for the movie Lieutenant Kijé. A troika is a Russian sleigh or carriage pulled by three horses.

LISTENING MAP *Raise your hand when the first two phrases (a and b) return in "Troika."*

Listening Map concept by Kay Greenhaw

SIMILAR PHRASES

These snowflakes are similar, but not the same. How are they different from one another?

Sometimes musical phrases are almost the same, or similar.

When you describe a form that has similar phrases, add a mark (ˈ) called a prime to the letter for the similar phrase. The form can be called a aˈ or b bˈ.

Is the phrase form a aˈ or a b in the first two lines of "Hi! Ho! The Rattlin' Bog"? Where does the difference occur?

IT'S A PITCH PUZZLE!

Are you ready for a puzzle? The first four phrases of " 'Way Down Yonder in the Brickyard" are all mixed up.

SING each phrase with pitch syllables.

a
do 'Way down yon-der in the brick-yard,

b'
do Re-mem-ber me.

a
do 'Way down yon-der in the brick-yard,

b
do Re-mem-ber me.

What is the correct order for the phrases, a b b' a or a b a b'?

NAME THOSE PITCHES!

You are listening to the radio, and you decide to join in the "Name Those Pitches" game. You try to recognize the mystery melody. It could be a melody with *mi so la* or one with *do re mi*.

How will you figure out the winning pitches? Listen carefully!

FROM POETRY TO PITCHES

Have you ever tried to set a poem to music?
That's what songwriters do all the time! This
activity may give you some ideas.

CREATE a melody for "I Wish."

Use the pitches shown with the lines of the
poem. Match them by color.

do   mi   so   la

do   do   re   mi

Here are more ideas for your melody! Include same, similar, and
different phrases. Try different
beginning and ending pitches.

Create an accompaniment for your melody with the instruments shown, or make your own special sounds on the words that have instrument pictures.

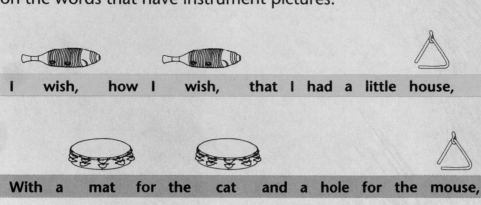

I wish, how I wish, that I had a little house,

With a mat for the cat and a hole for the mouse,

And a clock going "tock" in the corner of the room

And a kettle, and a cupboard, and a big birch broom.

THINK IT THROUGH

If you want to play your melody with a friend tomorrow, what are some ways you can remember it? Which way would work best for you?

Rhythms that Repeat

If you have a melody in mind, why not add some rhythms?
Try an **ostinato,** a pattern that repeats many times.

**CREATE a rhythm ostinato by repeating this pattern.
Snap the eighth notes and brush your hands for the
half notes.**

Two instruments can also share the ostinato.

maracas

güiro

**PERFORM the ostinato with the instru-
mental section of "I Let Her Go, Go."**

OSTINATO "TO GO"

You can add a playful movement ostinato to "I Let Her Go, Go."

FOLLOW the pictures to find out what to do each time you sing *go*.

1

I let her go, go,

2

Ee ay I let her go, go,

3

Ee ay I let her go

4

I let her go, go, go.

Meet
THE BARRA MACNEILS

The Barra MacNeils are from Nova Scotia, Canada. They perform traditional Celtic and Canadian music and write their own songs as well.

LISTEN to the Barra MacNeils discuss their music.

LISTENING

The Foxhunter's from *Flower Basket Medley*

Arranged by Sheumas, Kyle, Stewart, and Lucy MacNeil

Listen for the mouth music in "The Foxhunter's." Mouth music is created by singing very fast rhythms with nonsense syllables. It can be dance music when no instruments are handy. Try this mouth music.

die od-dle dee-dle i-dle did-dle-y i-dle dee-dle dum

Can you keep up with "The Foxhunter's"?

RHYTHMS HIT THE ROAD!

CREATE a dance of movement ostinatos. First, choose a pattern to perform with your feet.

Find a partner and teach one another your steps. Together, create an ostinato using both patterns. How many beats long is it?

PERFORM your ostinato to "The Foxhunter's."

MUSIC IS A WORLD WITHIN ITSELF

People all over the world enjoy music. The songs in this unit come from near and far.

Name each song pictured on the map, then name the country from which each song comes. Plan a travel route that includes all the orange countries.

SING the songs that come from these countries as you visit around the musical world.

Which songs are in $\frac{2}{4}$ meter? In $\frac{4}{4}$?

Which songs have phrases of different lengths? The same length?

CHECK IT OUT

1. How many phrases do you hear?

   a. two **b.** three **c.** four

2. Locate the rhythm pattern that is played. Which measure has the wrong number of beats?

   a. Measure 1 **b.** Measure 2 **c.** Measure 3 **d.** Measure 4

   Pattern 1

   Pattern 2

   Pattern 3

   Pattern 4

3. Which rhythm do you hear?

   a.

   b.

   c.

   d.

4. Which melody do you hear?

   a. do   **c.** do

   b. do   **d.** do

36

CREATE

Introduction in Eight

CREATE a melody. Use the pitches F G A C¹ D¹. Use this eight-beat rhythm pattern.

On a piece of paper, write your melody with the letters you find on the bells you chose.

The bell with the letter F sounds like *do*. Write your melody with pitch syllables, too.

If the meter signature of this rhythm pattern is ²/₄ , where do the bar lines go?

Play your melody as an introduction to "Fed My Horse."

Write

Stevie Wonder wrote "Sir Duke" in honor of jazz musician Duke Ellington. Think of a musician you admire.

Write a poem telling who the person is and why you look up to that person.

SONG OF THE WHALE

There is an animal so big that eight elephants could stand in a row on its back. Can you guess the name of this animal? It's the blue whale.

Sight is important to animals on land. In the dark ocean, however, sound is more important. Whales can hear very well. They signal one another with sound. The humpback whale produces the most musical sounds.

LISTENING

Whale Songs (excerpts from *And God Created Great Whales*)

by Alan Hovhaness

Listen to the song of the humpback whale. Do you hear any patterns that repeat?

DESCRIBE the tone color of their singing.

Pete Seeger, an American folk singer, wrote this song about the importance of protecting whales.

The Song of the World's Last Whale

Words and Music
by Peter Seeger

1. and 6. I heard the song___ of the world's last whale,___
2. It was down off Ber-mu-da___ Ear - ly last spring,___
(3.) did-n't just hear grunt-ing___ I did-n't just hear squeaks,___ I
4. Down in the Ant - arc-tic___ The___ har - poons wait,___
5. So here's a lit-tle test___ To see how you feel,___

As I rocked in the moon-light___ and reefed the
Near an un-der - wa-ter moun - tain___ Where the hump - backs
did-n't just hear___ bel - lows,___ I did-n't just hear
But it's up - on the land___ They de - cide my
Here's a lit - tle___ test for this age___ of the au-to - mo -

sail,___ It -'ll hap - pen to you al - so with - out
sing.___ I___ low - ered the mi - cro-phone A quar-ter mile___
shrieks.___ It was the mus - i - cal sing-ing And the pas-sion-ate
fate.___ In Lon - don Town They'll be tell- ing the
bile.___ If___ we___ can save___ Our sing -ers in the

fail, If it hap - pens to me___ sang the world's last whale.___
down, Switched___ on the re - cor-der And let the tape spin round.. 3. I
wail, That___ came from the heart___ Of the world's last whale.___
tale, If it's life or death For the world's last whale.___
sea, Per - haps___ there's a chance To save you and me.___

In the past, people living near the Arctic and Antarctic regions depended on whales. They used whale oil to heat their homes, the meat to feed their families, and the bones to make tools.

Once, there were thousands of whales in the seas. During the 1700s and 1800s, hunters from countries around the world killed many of them. Now, there are not many whales left. Many species of whales are threatened with extinction.

The narwhal is the most unusual-looking of all the whales. Its single, eight-foot-long white tusk is highly valued for its beauty. Narwhals are found in the waters around Greenland and other polar regions.

The Danish people who traveled to Greenland many years ago made recorders and furniture from narwhal tusks. Today, items are no longer made from these tusks. Strict international laws protect whales.

Variations on "English Nightingale"

by Jacob Van Eyck

Listen to music that might once have been played on a recorder made of narwhal tusk. Listen for the same melody played in different ways.

MEET
Eva Legêne

Eva Legêne is a world-famous recorder player. While she was living in Denmark in the late 1970s, she discovered two narwhal tusk recorders in the Rosenborg Castle in Copenhagen.

LISTEN to Eva Legêne talk about this important musical discovery.

TRAVELING ON

Roads Go Ever Ever On

Roads go ever ever on,
 Over rock and under tree,
By caves where never sun has shone,
 By streams that never find the sea;
Over snow by winter sown,
 And through the merry flowers of June,
Over grass and over stone,
 And under mountains in the moon.

Roads go ever ever on
 Under cloud and under star,
Yet feet that wandering have gone
 Turn at last to home afar.
Eyes that fire and sword have seen
 And horror in the halls of stone
Look at last on meadows green
 And trees and hills they long have known.

—J. R. R. Tolkien

43

HOME, SWEET HOME

Do you sing with your family or friends to pass the time on a trip? Cowboys sang on long cattle drives. They also sang at night to calm the herds, to keep away wild animals, and to ease loneliness.

SING "Trail to Mexico." Move your arm to show the shape of the melody.

TRAIL to MEXICO

American Cowboy Song
Music Adapted by Carol King

1. I made up my mind in the ear - ly morn
2. 'Twas in the year of eight - y - three
3. 'Twas in the spring - time of the year

To leave the home where I was born,
That A. J. Stin - son hired me.
I vol - un - teered to drive the steers.

To leave my na - tive home for a while,
He said, "Young man, I want you to go,
I'll tell you, boys, 'twas a long hard go,

And trav - el west for man - y a mile.
And fol - low my herd to Mex - i - co."
As the trail rolled on in - to Mex - i - co.

When you take a trip, your last stop is probably your home. Usually, the last pitch of a melody is a note called the home tone or **tonal center.** Ending on this note makes the melody sound finished.

ON YOUR WAY HOME

Children often make up their own words as they play a clapping game with this song. The words don't have to make much sense!

LISTEN to the song, then hum the tonal center.

FOUR WHITE HORSES

Caribbean Folk Song
Collected by Lois Choksy

Four white hors - es on the riv - er, Hey, hey, — hey, —

up to-mor-row, Up to-mor - row is a rain - y day.

Come on up— to the shal-low bay. Shal-low bay— is a

ripe ba - nan - a, Up to-mor - row is a rain - y day.

Melodies can have pitches higher and lower than the tonal center. Listen to a new song, "Down the Road." Which picture matches the melody of the last phrase?

1. tonal center

melody

melody

2. tonal center

melody

3. tonal center

A Story

Before radio and television were popular, songs like "The Old Carrion Crow" were passed from person to person. As you sing, see how the clear story, repeated melodies, and funny nonsense syllables could make this song easy to remember.

The Old Carrion Crow

Nova Scotian Folk Song

Verse *mf*

1. Oh, the old car-rion crow was sit-ting on an oak,
2. Hur-ry now bring me my cross and my bow,
3. Oh, the tai-lor shot and missed his mark,
4. The old sow died and the bells did toll,
5. Oh, now the old sow's dead and gone,

Fol the rid-dle, all the rid-dle hey ding

(1.) doh,
(2.) doh,
(3.) doh, And he
(4.) doh, And the
(5.) doh, And the

48

in a Song

(1.) Watch - ing a tai - lor cut - ting out a coat.
(2.) That I may shoot yon car - ri - on_____ crow.
(3.) shot the mil - ler's sow right through____ the_____ heart.
(4.) lit - tle pigs_____ cried and prayed____ for her soul.
(5.) lit - tle pigs_____ play and wad - dle_____ on,

mp *slightly held back* *in tempo*

Sing he, sing ho, the old car - rion crow, Fol the rid - dle, all the rid - dle

Refrain *slightly held back*

hey ding doh. Ki - me - lea - ro kill my kea - ro, ki - me - lea - ro ki - mo,

in tempo

To me bump, bump, bump, jump Pol - ly wol - ly lee, Lin - ko kil - ly cum ki - mo.

FOL-THE-RIDDLE RHYTHMS

Here's a chance to practice some new rhythms.

CLAP the beat and pat each rhythm. How many sounds to a beat do you hear?

fol the rid - dle   kil - ly cum   cum kil - ly

hey ding   doh

PERFORM a new rhythmic phrase by reading this pattern.

kil - ly cum kil - ly cum kil - ly cum doh

fol the rid - dle cum kil - ly hey ding doh

 Karşi Bar *Turkish Dance*
LISTENING

 LISTEN for the rhythmic phrase shown above. Then dance to the music.

SING and pat the rhythm for each instrument.

piti, piti, piti, el pitío

ton, ton, ton, el tambor

tara, tara, tara, la guitarra

Which word patterns in the song match these rhythms?

lin, lin, lin, el violín

THINK IT THROUGH

What are some ways you could use the rhythm patterns or parts of the patterns to create other rhythm patterns?

MEET THE
INSTRUMENTS

You might see musical instruments among the odds and ends for sale at a flea market or fair. You will name quite a collection of instruments by singing this cumulative song!

En la feria de San Juan
In the Market of San Juan

Puerto Rican Folk Song
English Version by MMH

Verse

G   D 7

Spanish: En la fe - ria de San Juan, yo com - pré un pi -
Pronunciation: en la fe ɾya ðe san xwan yo kom pɾe un pi
English: In the mar - ket of San Juan, I— bought my - self a

Repeat this section, adding an instrument vocally each time

G   D 7   G

tí - o, pi - ti, pi - ti, pi - ti, el pi - tí - o.
ti o pi ti pi ti pi ti el pi ti o
whis - tle, *(whistle the melody)*———— the whis - tle.

Refrain

D   C   G   D 7   G

Ven - ga u - sted, ven - ga u - sted, a la fe - ria de San Juan,
ßeng gau steð ßeng gau steð a la fe ɾya ðe san xwan
Come with me, come with me, to the mar - ket of San Juan.

D   C   G   D 7   G

Ven - ga u - sted, ven - ga u - sted, a la fe - ria de San Juan.
ßeng gau steð ßeng gau steð a la fe ɾya ðe san xwan
Come with me, come with me, to the mar - ket of San Juan.

2. En la feria de San Juan
   yo compré un tambor.
   Ton, ton, ton, el tambor, . . .

   en la fe ɾya ðe san xwan
   yo kom pɾe un tam boɾ
   ton ton ton el tam boɾ . . .

   In the market of San Juan
   I bought myself a drum.
   Tum, tum, tum, tum, the drum . . .

3. yo compré una guitarra,
   tara, tara, tara, la guitarra . . .

   yo kom pɾe una gi ta ɾa
   ta ɾa ta ɾa ta ɾa la gi ta ɾa . . .

   I bought a guitar,
   tara, tara, tara, the guitar . . .

4. yo compré un violín,
   Lin, lin, lin, el violín, . . .

   yo kom pɾe un ßyo lin
   lin lin lin el ßyo lin . . .

   I bought a violin,
   Lin, lin, lin, the violin, . . .

FAMILIES OF INSTRUMENTS

When you see a family picture, you might enjoy comparing the faces you see. Look at the **orchestral** families below. How are the instruments in each picture alike?

trumpet

tuba

French horn

trombone

BRASS FAMILY

double bass

harp

cello

violin

viola

STRING FAMILY

snare drum

cymbals

triangle

tambourine

timpani

xylophone

piano

bass drum

PERCUSSION FAMILY

piccolo

flute

clarinet

alto saxophone

bassoon

English horn

oboe

WOODWIND FAMILY

Spotlight on MODEST MUSSORGSKY

Modest Petrovich Mussorgsky (1839–1881) studied piano with his mother. He began composing short pieces in school. Then he became busy with a military career and didn't get further musical training. His rich harmony and expressive ideas, however, place him among the most talented Russian composers. Mussorgsky wrote Pictures at an Exhibition *to go with ten paintings by a friend.*

LISTENING

Promenade
from *Pictures at an Exhibition*
by *Modest Mussorgsky*

An art exhibition is a display of art. As you listen to Promenade, *imagine that you are walking and looking at paintings.*

LISTEN for the instrument families that play this melody.

LISTENING MAP *Tap each footprint as you listen for the entrance of each instrument family.*

Listening Map concept by Melody A. Long

Symbols and Cymbals

The musical symbols for four equal sounds to a beat can be written with four **sixteenth notes** ( ) .

Fol the rid - dle, all the rid - dle hey ding doh.

Three unequal sounds to a beat can be written with two sixteenth notes and one eighth note (or) .

Lin - ko kil - ly cum ki - mo.

MAKE UP words with three unequal sounds to a beat.

Listen for beats with three or four sounds in "Karşi Bar."

Look at the notes below. Part of the rhythmic phrase from "Karşi Bar" is missing.

| kil - ly cum | kil - ly cum | kil - ly cum | doh |

| fol the rid - dle | | hey ding | doh |
| cum kil - ly | | | |

POINT to the rhythm that belongs in the empty box.

How did you decide on your answer?

From left to right, the kanun, oud, tez, dumbek, and ney are heard in traditional Turkish music.

PAT the rhythm of the green line. Then sing the line as an ostinato.

TRAIL TO MEXICO

American
Cowboy Song
Music Adapted by
Carol King

do

G   C   G   C

1. I made up my mind _____ in the ear - ly
2. 'Twas in the _____ year _____ of __ eight - y -
3. 'Twas in the _____ spring - time _____ of the

Vocal Ostinato

do

Rid - in' on the West-ern Trail.

D7   G

morn _____ To   leave   the
three _____ That   A.   J.
year _____ I   vol - un -

Up   in   the   sad - dle   all   day.

'G

home _____ where _ I was born, _____ To leave my
Stin - son hired _ me. _____ He said,"Young
teered _____ to - drive the steers. _____ I'll tell you,

Rid - in' on the West-ern Trail.   Up in the sad-dle all day.

na - tive home for a
man, I want you to
boys, 'twas a long hard

Rid - in' on the West - ern Trail.

while, And trav - el
go, And fol - low my
go, As the trail rolled

Up in the sad - dle all day.

west for man-y a mile.
herd to Mex - i - co."
on in-to Mex - i - co.

Rid-in' on the West-ern Trail. Up in the sad-dle all day.

Music that begins *before* the first beat of a measure begins on an **upbeat.** Look before the first bar line. When a song starts with an upbeat, there are fewer beats before the first bar line than are shown in the meter signature. Which part of "Trail to Mexico" begins with an upbeat, the melody or the ostinato?

MOVING

This song may bring some bounce to your steps!
As you sing the melody, notice how it moves
down to pitches below *do*.

DOWN THE ROAD

American Folk Song

A

G   D7   G

Down the road, ___ down the road, ___

G   D7   G

Come a-long and walk to-geth-er down the road! ___

B

Ev'-ry time I get the blues, ___ I walk the soles right off my shoes. ___

Don't know why I get so blue, ___ But walk-ing car-ries me right on through.

In "Down the Road," you sang two pitches that are "down the road" from *do*.

FIND *do re mi*. **Do is the tonal center of this song. Where are the new pitches?**

The new pitches are called *low so* and *low la*. Recall the pitch syllables you have learned.

The introductions are not yet over! Each pitch has a letter name as well as a pitch syllable name.

treble clef

G →

D E   G A B

C D E F G A B C

The letter names of the pitches in "Down the Road" are D E G A B.

SING **"Down the Road" with letter names.**

The **treble clef** is shaped like an old-fashioned letter G. It circles the second staff line, and a note on that line is called G.

HIT THE TRAIL

Now you can sing this ostinato three different ways.

SING it with pitch syllables, letter names, and words.

Vocal Ostinato

Rid-in' on the West-ern Trail.   Up   in the sad-dle all day.

THINK IT THROUGH

Listen to "Trail to Mexico" with and without the ostinato. How does the ostinato change the song? Why would a composer add an ostinato to a song?

SING AND CLAP A PATTERN

Clap own hands.

Clap partner's hands.

Review a song you know.

RAISE your hand when you hear this pattern in "Four White Horses."

do   la₁   so₁

Play the game in groups of four.

Clap own hands.

Clap side partner's hands.

SWITCH TO SWAPPING

What does "swap" mean to you? In this song, the swapping goes on and on!

LISTEN to the song and find all the items that are swapped along the way.

SWAPPING SONG

Appalachian Folk Song

Verse

1. When I was a lit - tle boy I lived by my - self; ___
2. Rats ___ and the mice, ___ they ___ led me such a life, I
3. Roads ___ were so long ___ and the lanes were so nar - row, I
4. Wheel - bar - row broke ___ and my wife got a fall; ___
5. Swapped my wheel - bar - row and ___ got me a horse; ___

All the bread and cheese I had, I put it on the shelf. ___
had to go to Lon - don to ___ get my - self a wife.
had to bring her home ___ in an old ___ wheel - bar - row.
Down ___ came the wheel - bar - row, wife and all. ___
Then ___ I rode from ___ cross ___ to ___ cross.

Refrain

Wing wong wad-dle, to my jack straw strad-dle, To my

John-nie fair fad-dle, to my long ways home.

6. Swapped my horse and got me a mare;
   Then I rode from fair to fair.

7. Swapped my mare and got me a mule;
   Then I rode like a doggone fool.

8. Swapped my mule and got me a goat;
   When I got on him, he wouldn't tote.

9. Swapped my goat and got me a sheep;
   Then I rode myself to sleep.

10. Swapped my sheep and got me a cow;
    And in that trade I just learned how.

11. Swapped my cow and got me a calf;
    In that trade I just lost half.

12. Swapped my calf and got me a hen;
    Oh what a pretty thing I had then.

13. Swapped my hen and got me a rat;
    Put it on the haystack away from
    the cat.

14. Swapped my rat and got me a mouse;
    Its tail caught afire and burned up
    my house.

NAME and point to the tonal center of this song.

You can read *all* the pitches and rhythms in this song!

Return to Rhythms

Can you remember the missing phrases of "The Old Carrion Crow"?

Oh, the old carrion crow was sitting on an oak,

_____,

Watching a tailor cutting out a coat.
Sing he, sing ho, the old carrion crow,

_____.

Kimelearo kill my kearo, kimelearo kimo,
To me bump, bump, bump, jump Polly wolly lee,

_____.

Add a personal touch to this folk song! Replace the traditional nonsense words with these rhythm patterns.

PERFORM a different pattern with each verse.

step

snap

pat

clap

clap

70

A scene from a performance of *Carmen* at the San Francisco Opera.

LISTENING

Prelude (excerpt) from *Carmen*
by Georges Bizet

*An **overture**, or prelude, is an instrumental piece that begins an opera or other large musical work. The overture settles the audience and may introduce musical ideas that will be heard.*

TAP the coins on the beat from left to right as you listen to the prelude to *Carmen*.

How many beats are in each phrase? How many phrases did you hear?

*Each phrase of this prelude begins with a rhythmic **motive**. A motive is a short pattern used often in a piece of music. Which pattern shows the motive?*

RHYTHM SWAP

Have you ever swapped baseball cards or video games with a friend? In this game, you will create patterns by swapping the rhythms in the railroad cars.

Work with a partner and choose different sounds to perform the rhythms. Each partner chooses a pattern from one side. Perform the patterns one after the other. Then, swap the order of the patterns and perform them that way.

An **interlude** is a short musical connection between sections or verses of a longer musical piece.

PERFORM your two patterns as an interlude between two verses of "Swapping Song."

Here's a song you know. How can
you figure out what song it is without hearing it?

SING the song when you recognize it.

THE FORM

In music, you hear repetition and contrast. Some phrases are the same. Some are different. This is also true of larger parts of musical works.

Some music is made up of two or more sections. Songs with two sections that sound the same have a form called A A. Songs with two different-sounding sections have a form called A B.

NAME the form of the song "Down the Road." Why did you choose your answer?

In a Mountain Path

Traditional Chinese Song Arranged by Han Kuo-huang

"In a Mountain Path" is a Chinese song played by a modern Chinese orchestra. The modern Chinese orchestra is divided into bowed strings, plucked strings, woodwinds, and percussion. How are these families different from the families of the symphony orchestra?

Music from China, a modern ensemble, playing typical Chinese instruments.

What are some things you hear in this song?

RAISE your hand when the A section returns. Then improvise a dance to the music.

Unusual limestone hills near the city of Kuei-lin in southern China.

LANDSCAPE IN THE STYLE OF DONG BEIYUAN

This Chinese scroll was painted in the time of the Ming Dynasty (1368–1644). The word *Ming* means "bright" in Chinese. Can you see how the artist, Dong Qichang, used contrasts to make his ink painting interesting and dramatic?

GETTING THERE IS HALF THE FUN

Do you like sending postcards? Think of the song shown on one of these cards. Describe what you might see if you went to the place in the song. Then sing the song.

Choose your favorite card and write a message on a piece of paper to friends "back home." Tell them about the rhythm, pitches, or game that goes with the song on the postcard.

CHECK IT OUT

1. Which rhythm do you hear?

2. Which rhythm do you hear?

3. Which pitches do you hear?

a.

c.

b.

d.

4. Which pitches do you hear?

a.

c.

b.

d.

CREATE

Pair Up for ABA

CREATE a melody with a partner. Use the pitches
D E G A B and one of the rhythm patterns below.

PERFORM your melody as part
of a B section between the
verses of "Trail to Mexico."

Write

The journey to a place can be as
interesting as the place you visit.

Write words for a song describing
your trip to the Market of San Juan
or on a cattle drive to Mexico.
Describe what you see, what you
think, who you meet, and what
surprises or difficulties occur along
the way.

Encore
BLUE SKIES

Songs, poems, and stories about rain are found in cultures all over the world. What feeling does this song express about rain? How do you feel when it rains?

SINGIN' in the RAIN

Music by Nacio Herb Brown
Words by Arthur Freed

I'm sing - in' in the rain, just sing - in' in the rain;

What a glo - ri - ous feel - ing, I'm hap - py a - gain!

I'm laugh - ing at clouds so dark up a - bove.

The sun's in my heart and I'm read - y for love.

GRAY SKIES

Gene Kelly, an American actor and dancer, made the song "Singin' in the Rain" famous in the movie of the same name.

G
Let the storm - y clouds chase ev' - ry - one— from the place;

G **D7**
Come on— with the rain, I've a smile— on my face!

D7
I'll walk down the lane with a hap - py re - frain,

D7 **G**
And sing - in',— just sing - in' in— the rain!—

A FOLKTALE FROM KENYA

In the plains of Kenya, in Africa, where the land is dry,
herders are always hoping for rain. Without it, the people
and animals cannot survive. The Nandi people of Kenya
tell the following tale.

*O*nce there was a young cowherd who was very skilled
with the bow and arrow. One summer there had been
no rain, and the weather was very hot and dry. The
cows had no water to drink. The cows also had nothing
to eat because the grass had shriveled up and died.

One day the cowherd saw an eagle flying high above.
As the eagle flew over him, a beautiful feather fell at his
feet. The cowherd eagerly picked up the feather and
saw that it would make a fine addition to his arrow.

The cowherd shot the arrow into a large cloud that was
gathering above the plain. Suddenly, there was light-
ning and thunder. The cloud burst and rain poured
down. The long drought had ended. The cows were no
longer thirsty, and the grass grew high and green again.

CHOOSE instrument sounds for each part of the
story. Tell the story with sounds.

SING the following vocal call as an introduction
and coda to the story.

Call   *Response*   3

Please bring us,   please bring us,   bring us some rain.

Rainfall *by Linda Worsley*

People have dreamed of controlling the weather for thousands of years. Inventors have tried to make artificial rain. People living in dry areas held rain dances in the hope of rainfall.

MOVE to music that sounds like rain.

Cleo Parker Robinson, an American dancer, created her own rain dance.

Members of Cleo Parker Robinson's troupe rehearse "Raindance."

Meet CLEO PARKER ROBINSON

Cleo Parker Robinson has made her career as a choreographer, a person who creates dances. She trained in both modern dance and ballet. Robinson formed her own dance school while she was a college student. She has traveled with her dancers around the world and has received many awards for her teaching and community service. One of her goals is to make the experience of dance available to all.

LISTEN to Cleo Parker Robinson talk about her experiences performing her rain dance.

Just Imagine

I Wonder

I wonder how it feels to fly
high in the sky . . .
    like a bird.
I wonder how it feels to sit
on a nest . . .
    like a bird.
I wonder how it feels to catch
a worm in the morning . . .
    like a bird.
I feel funny . . .
maybe he is wondering
    how it feels to be like a man.

—Earl Thompson (Yakima)

MOVING MELODIES

How do you feel when it rains?

TRACE the shape of the melody in the air while you sing the song.

I Don't Care If the Rain Comes Down

American Folk Song

A
I don't care if the rain comes down, I'm gon - na dance all day,

I don't care if the rain comes down, I'm gon - na dance all day.

B
Hey, hey, car - ry me a - way, I'm gon - na dance all day,

Hey, hey, car - ry me a - way, I'm gon - na dance all day.

Melodies can move in three ways.

Some move with **repeated notes,** using one pitch that is repeated.

I   don't   care   if   the   rain   comes   down

They can move by **steps.** Each note is followed by a pitch just above or below it.

I   don't   care   if   the   rain   comes   down

When a melody moves by **skips,** each note is followed by a pitch two or more steps away.

I   don't   care   if   the   rain   comes   down

MOVE to the repeated notes, steps, and skips in these melodies.

Listen for repeated notes, steps, and skips in the melody of this song.

La pájara pinta
THE SPECKLED BIRD

Mexican Folk Song
English Version
by MMH

Spanish: Y es- ta- ba la pá- ja- ra pin- ta sen- ta- da en su ver- de li-
Pronunciation: yes ta βa la pa xa ɾa pin ta sen ta ðaen su βeɾ ðe li
English: A bright speck- led bird— was sit- ting up- on a green lem- on

món.— Con el pi- co re- co- ge las flo- res, Con el
mon kon el pi ko ɾe ko xe las flo ɾes kon el
branch.— With her beak— she gath- ered flow- ers, with her

pi- co re- co- ge el a- mor.— Ay, ay, ay, ay! ¿En
pi ko ɾe ko xel a moɾ ai ai ai ai en
beak— she gath- ered love,— Ay, ay, ay, ay— Then

dón- de la en- cuen- tro yo?— Con el pi- co re- co- ge las
don de laen kwen tɾo yo kon el pi ko ɾe ko xe las
tell me where will it be?— With her beak— she gath- ered

flo- res, Con el pi- co re- co- ge el a- mor.—
flo ɾes kon el pi ko ɾe ko xel a moɾ
flow- ers, with her beak— she gath- ered love.—

This song is about the workers who load cargo onto ships. Sometimes, ship captains treated these workers unfairly.

SIGNAL to show how the melody moves. Does it move mostly by repeated notes, steps, or skips?

PAY ME MY MONEY DOWN

African American Work Song
from the Georgia Sea Islands
Collected and Adapted by Lydia A. Parrish

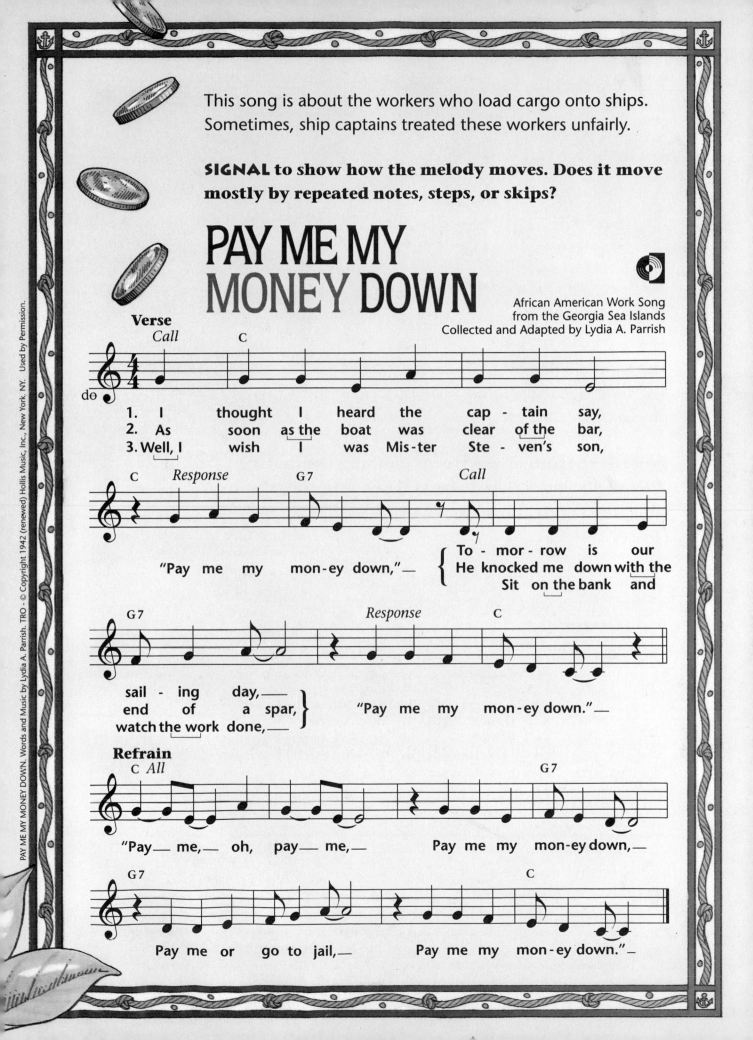

Verse
Call

C

do

1. I thought I heard the cap - tain say,
2. As soon as the boat was clear of the bar,
3. Well, I wish I was Mis - ter Ste - ven's son,

C *Response*   G7   *Call*

"Pay me my mon-ey down,"—

{ To - mor - row is our
  He knocked me down with the
  Sit on the bank and

G7   *Response*   C

sail - ing day,—
end of a spar, }   "Pay me my mon-ey down."—
watch the work done,—

Refrain
C *All*   G7

"Pay— me,— oh, pay— me,— Pay me my mon-ey down,—

G7   C

Pay me or go to jail,— Pay me my mon-ey down."—

AN OLD STORY

This song is based on a Biblical story. Noah saves some animals from a flood by loading them onto a boat called an ark.

PAT the rhythm of the words and sing the motive *There's one more river to cross.* **Then sing the whole song and create more verses.**

ONE MORE RIVER

Nineteenth Century
College Song

Verse F   C7

1. Old   No-ah, he   built him-self an ark;
2. The   an - i - mals went in   one   by one;
3. The   an - i - mals went in   two   by two;   } There's one more riv-er to
4. The   an - i - mals went in   three by three;
5. The   an - i - mals went in   four by four;

F

cross. {
He   built   it   out   of   hick' - ry bark;
The   el - e - phant chew-ing a   car - a - way bun;
The rhi - no - cer - os and the kang - a - roo;   } There's
The   bear,   the   bug, and the bum - ble - bee;
The   hip - po - po - ta - mus stuck in   the door;

92

one more riv - er to cross. There's one more riv - er, And

that wide riv - er is Jor - dan, There's one more

riv - er, There's one more riv - er to cross.____

6. The animals went in five by five;
   There's one more river to cross.
   "It's raining," said Noah, "so look alive!"
   There's one more river to cross.
   Refrain

7. The animals went in six by six; . . .
   The monkeys were up to monkey tricks; . . .
   Refrain

8. The animals went in sev'n by sev'n; . . .
   The rabbit said, "I wish I had driv'n.". . .
   Refrain

9. The animals went in eight by eight; . . .
   "That's 'nuff," said Noah, and slammed
      the gate! . . .
   Refrain

10. And as they talked of this and that; . . .
    The ark, it bumped on Ararat; . . .
    Refrain

DISCOVER BEAT DIVISIONS

Clap this motive while you walk with the beat. How many sounds are there to each beat?

| one | | more | riv - | er | to | cross |

The arks show the number of sounds to each beat.

MATCH each row to one of the beats shown above.

no sound to the beat	
one sound to the beat	
two unequal sounds to the beat	
three equal sounds to the beat	

CLAP the rhythms of these words. Then match them with the patterns of arks.

caraway bun

stuck in the door

kangaroo

one by one

Many beats in "Come and Sing Together" are divided into two parts.

LISTEN to discover if the beats are divided equally or unequally.

COME AND SING TOGETHER

Hungarian Melody

If you'd dance then you must have boots of shin-ing leath - er,

Mon - ey in your pock - et - book, in your hat a feath - er.

But if you would sing with me,

you don't need a cent, you see, so come and sing to-geth - er!

If you'd dance then you must have boots of shin-ing leath - er!

SPOTLIGHT ON
Maria Teresa Carreño

Maria Teresa Carreño (1853–1917) was a child prodigy. Some people even called her another Mozart. She was born in Caracas, Venezuela, and gave her first piano concert in New York City when she was eight years old. When she was about ten, "Teresita" played for President Abraham Lincoln and his family.

Carreño was best known as a concert pianist. As an adult, she also directed and sang in operas, composed, and conducted. Her energy and enthusiasm were amazing.

LISTENING

Scherzo (excerpt) from String Quartet in B Minor
by Teresa Carreño

When do you hear three equal sounds to a beat? Two equal sounds to a beat?

In this photograph of a string quartet, which instruments of the string family do you see? Are they producing sound by bowing or plucking the strings?

LISTENING MAP   *Listen for the sounds of bowed (arco) and plucked (pizzicato) strings.*

KEY

= $\frac{6}{8}$ ($\stackrel{2}{\cdot}$) arco, allegro, staccato   = $\frac{2}{4}$ arco, slower, legato

= $\frac{2}{4}$ pizzicato   = $\frac{6}{8}$ ($\stackrel{2}{\cdot}$) arco, slower, staccato

START

SOLOS   DUET   SOLOS and DUETS

violin   violin   violin

cello   cello   cello

slow down

viola   violin

solo   solo

slow down

high solo   solo

Flying with the Eagles

What do you think of when you see an eagle fly?

Dynamics are the levels of loudness and softness of the performance. How do the dynamics in this song help express feelings?

THE EAGLE

Music by Hap Palmer
Words by Martha Cheney

cresc. v.2 only

mf 1. Born   for a west-ern sky, ___   sweep-ing a cir-cle
mp 2. Brave   and a hunt-er's son, ___   *f* the land was his 'til he
p 3. There   on a moun-tain high, ___   wound-ed ___ ea-gle
mf 4. Dream-   ing of days gone by, ___   when lit-tle chil-dren

as   he flies. ___
met   a gun. ___
wants   to die. ___   } He was free ___ when they let him be. ___
watched him fly. ___

98

SING the song with dynamics that are different from the recording. Find another way to express the feelings of the words.

Among many Native American cultures, the eagle is admired for its beauty, grace, and strength. The eagle is also a spiritual figure to many Native Americans, serving as a messenger between people and the Creator. The eagle has the sharpest eyes, flies the highest, and carries prayers on its feathers up to the Creator.

MEET JULIUS CHAVEZ

Julius Chavez is a Native American of the Navajo nation in Arizona and New Mexico. He has spent many years learning songs and dances of the Navajo people. He is also interested in learning and teaching the music of other Native American groups.

The songs and dances are passed on from performer to performer and from parents to children. One must listen carefully to learn the songs, because they are not written down. Mr. Chavez learned much of what he knows from his grandparents.

LISTEN as Julius Chavez explains the meaning of "A'tsah Biyiin Sin."

A'tsah Biyiin Sin

Traditional Laguna Melody
Words by Julius Chavez

In "A'tsah Biyiin Sin," (The Song that Belongs to the Eagle) Julius Chavez uses the melody from the traditional Laguna Eagle Dance Song with his own words in Navajo. The dance shows scenes in the eagle's life, which may teach people about their own lives.

LISTEN to "A'tsah Biyiin Sin."

LISTENING

101

YOUR TURN WITH DYNAMICS

Have you ever watched a fire in a fireplace, or a campfire?
Fire is a very powerful natural force. Poets have written
about fire as if it had a personality and feelings. This poem
was written by a thirteen-year-old girl from England.

READ the poem. What is fire's enemy?

FIRE

*I am fire. You know me
For my warmth and light
For my crackling, leaping
Colored light
Which comforts all.
I am fire. You know me
For my endless moving,
Burning, destroying hunger
Which eats all.
I am fire. I have one foe
Who conquers my might,
Who quenches my thirst,
Who swallows my light.*

—Pat Taylor

THINK IT THROUGH

How could you use sound and movement to show a fire? How could you
show the fire growing? Dying down?

CHOOSE the dynamics and movement you feel would best express the meaning of the poem. Speak the poem with dynamics and perform your movement.

CANAL

The American artist Helen Frankenthaler often paints shapes of color that let each viewer see something different in them. What do you see in this painting?

Sing All Day

Look closely at the pitches of "I Don't Care If the Rain Comes Down." Where is the new pitch?

I don't care if the rain comes down, I'm gon-na sing all day,

I don't care if the rain comes down, I'm gon-na sing all day.

Fa is the pitch syllable between *mi* and *so.* Name these syllables from low to high, then sing the verse with pitch syllables.

so₁ la₁ do re mi fa so la

SING the two melodic motives on the next page. Try the motions!

Motive 1

Touch shoulders.

Touch head.

Shake hands overhead.

Motive 2

Touch shoulders.

Touch waist.

Touch knees.

LISTENING

Volte *by Michael Praetorius*

 The volte was a popular dance in European courts in the early 1600s. What kind of movement does this music make you want to do?

MOVE to the motives as you listen to "Volte." Then play each motive on resonator bells. C and F are the new letter names.

CONCERT CHAMPÊTRE

Musicians of Praetorius' time enjoyed playing various combinations of instruments. This painting shows early keyboard, string, and wind instruments.

Spotlight on
MICHAEL PRAETORIUS

Michael Praetorius (1571–1621) was a scholar and a musician. He wrote many important books on church music, composition, performance, and musical instruments.

Praetorius' woodcut illustrations of Renaissance instruments were very detailed. Many historical instruments could be rebuilt much later by using his pictures as guides. His pictures include the string instruments above and the organ at right.

Praetorius worked as an organist for most of his life. He made collections of his own pieces and arrangements. His work made him a rich man, and when he died he left all his money to the poor.

Step to the Ark!

In the song "One More River," the animals did the walking. Now you can "step to the ark"! Before you move, look at the notation for each rhythm.

CLAP the rhythm of each word several times.

cross

hip - po

el - e - phant

BY TWO OR BY SIX?

The meter signature of "One More River" can be written in two ways, ²ₚ and ⁶/₈. Although these two meter signatures look different, each measure lasts as long as two **dotted quarter notes** (♩. ♩.) or **six eighth notes** (♫♫♫ ♫♫♫).

FIND the meter signature and ♫♫♫ pattern in "One More River" on page 92. Learn the dance.

Form arches; first couple walks under.

Each couple follows the first couple.

CLAP and speak the rhythm pattern below. Say *cross,* *hippo,* and *elephant* for the three rhythms.

U.S. Marine Band

 LISTENING

Over the Hills and Far Away (excerpt)

by Percy Grainger

This march was written by Percy Grainger for a military concert band in 1918. Unlike the orchestra, the concert band has only three families of instruments: woodwinds, brass, and percussion. Which family of instruments is not in a concert band?

LISTEN for the rhythms above in the march.

SPOTLIGHT ON
Percy Grainger

*P*ercy Aldridge Grainger (1882–1961) was an Australian composer and pianist. His mother gave him his first piano lessons, and he began his concert career at the age of ten.

One of Grainger's favorite foods was brown-sugar sandwiches. Because he didn't like carrying things, he tied his pens, pencils, and papers to his jacket with string. He also planned his own museum, including the donation of his own skeleton!

Grainger was known as a fine pianist. He also became an important scholar of English folk music, researching and collecting English songs, many of which he wove into his own new compositions.

ADD A LITTLE HARMONY

In this song the b'y, or boy, is a busy young fisherman from Newfoundland, an island off the east coast of Canada.

I's the B'y

Newfoundland Folk Song

Verse

1. I's the b'y that builds the boat, And I's the b'y that sails her!
2. Sods and rinds to cov-er your flake,___ Cakes and tea for sup-per,
3. I don't want your mag-got-y fish,___ That's no good for win-ter,

I's the b'y that catch-es the fish, And brings them home to Liz-er.
Cod-fish in the spring o' the year,___ Fried in mag-got-y but-ter.
I could buy as good___ as that___ Down in Bon-a-vis-ta.

Refrain

Hip your part-ner, Sal-ly Tib-bo, Hip your part-ner, Sal-ly Brown!

Fo-go, Twil-lin-gate, Mor-ton's Har-bour, All a-round the cir-cle.

112

In "I's the B'y," *do* appears in the first space. What is the letter name for *do*?

The **key signature** comes before the meter signature at the beginning of a song. When *do* is F, the key signature has a **flat** (♭) on the third line.

Harmony is created when two or more different pitches are sung or played at the same time. Try singing *do* in harmony with "I's the B'y."

CREATE another harmony by singing this pattern with the song. Clap lightly with each *do*, pat with each low *so*.

THINK IT THROUGH

Which do you prefer for this song, harmony with pitches that stay the same or harmony with pitches that change? Why?

La raspa
Mexican Folk Music

"La raspa" (The Rasp) is a popular Mexican folk dance.

MATCH the harmonic pattern you hear in this dance with one of the patterns below.

HEARING HARMONY

Find your favorite harmony for "Pay Me My Money Down."
As you hear harmony that stays on the same pitch, predict
where harmony changes would sound better.

**COMPARE these harmony changes with your
predictions.**

How many times would you need to play this harmonic
pattern to accompany the song? Which other piece in this
lesson has similar harmony changes?

Dancers of the
Ballet Folklórico
of Mexico City.

THE DRAMA OF DYNAMICS

What does the word *dynamic* mean to you? It can mean constant activity and change.

In music, the dynamics are the changes in loudness and softness. Here are some common dynamic markings found in music.

f	**forte**	loud
mf	**mezzo forte**	medium loud
mp	**mezzo piano**	medium soft
p	**piano**	soft
$<$	**crescendo**	gradually get louder
$>$	**decrescendo**	gradually get softer

A DYNAMIC BAND

A wide range of dynamics is possible with a concert band. Not only can each instrument be played loudly or softly, but also different combinations of instruments can sound louder or softer.

LISTENING MAP *Listen for the dynamics in "Over the Hills and Far Away." The markings show you what to expect.*

1 Introduction *mp*
2 **A** *pp*
3 **A** *pp*
4 **B** *pp* <
5 **B** *p*
6 **A** *mp*
7 **A** *mp* <
8 **B** *mf*
9 **B** *f* <
10 **A** *mf* <
11 **A** *f* <
12 **B** *ff* <
13 **B** *fff*

THINK IT THROUGH

If *f* (forte) means loud, what do you think *ff* and *fff* mean? How do the dynamic changes affect the way you feel?

SINGING WITH DYNAMICS

"Come and Sing Together" tells of folk dancing in Hungary, a country in Europe where such songs and dances have been passed down for generations. Today, dances are seen at village celebrations of holidays and weddings, accompanied by live music and singing.

SING the first part of the song and follow the dynamic markings. Try singing it in two parts. Can you still hear the dynamic changes?

COME AND SING *Together*

Hungarian Melody

mp
Dm
do — If you'd dance then you must have boots of shin-ing leath - er,

do — If you'd dance then you must have boots of shin-ing

mp
Dm
Mon -ey in your pock - et -book, in your hat a feath - er.

mp
leath - er, Mon - ey in your pock - et - book, in your hat a

119

A METER MYSTERY

The meter signature is missing from the music below.

LISTEN and follow the music. Think about how you can tell what the meter signature should be.

The rhythm has many clues. Clues: How many beats do you feel in a set, or measure? How many sounds to each beat do you hear? Are the beats divided equally or unequally?

What is the meter signature of this song?

WHICH RHYTHM?

"La raspa" has rhythms made for dancing! The music shifts back and forth between two sections, A and B. In each section you hear one rhythmic motive more than any other.

In which section do you hear ♩♩♩♩ many times? In which do you hear ♩ ♪? Try the motions to each motive, then listen for them again.

BAILE EN TEHUANTEPEC

When Mexican artist Diego Rivera traveled to the Tehuantepec region of Mexico, he sketched hundreds of scenes, some of which he turned into paintings years later. In this painting, the people are dancing to lively Mexican folk music.

Los Angeles County Museum of Art

DANCE TO LA RASPA!

La raspa means "the rasp," a tool used to smooth the rough places on metal. In the dance for "La raspa," the hands and feet move back and forth like a rasp. The dance is sometimes known as the Mexican Hat Dance because it can be danced around a hat placed on the floor.

1 Find a partner.

2 Move to the music.

4 Skip, gallop, or slide and find a new partner.

3 Swing your partner.

EXPRESSIVE MOMENTS

Music can express the way a singer or songwriter feels about something, from calm to angry, from amused to serious.

What are some feelings expressed by the songs pictured here?

SING your favorite song from the unit. Sing it expressively.

CHECK IT OUT

1. How does this melody move?

   a. steps and skips   **c.** repeated notes, steps, and skips

   b. mostly skips   **d.** repeated notes and steps

2. Which example do you hear?

   a.   **c.**

   b.   **d.**

3. Which melody do you hear?

   a.   **c.**

   b.   **d.**

4. Which rhythm do you hear?

   a.

   b.

   c.

   d.

CREATE

Snappy Interludes

CREATE an eight-beat pattern. Use each word and rhythm at least once. On a piece of paper, write your pattern.

cross   hip - po   el - e- phant

The boxes below will help you plan your patterns.

$\frac{6}{8}$ ☐ ☐ ☐ ☐ ☐ ☐ ☐ cross

PERFORM the pattern twice through as an interlude between the verses of "One More River."

Write

Choose a person, bird, or animal from one of the songs in this unit.

Write a diary entry describing how the person, bird, or animal you chose feels about what happens in the song.

ENCORE Melodies

Traditionally, most Native American music is sung, accompanied by rattles and drums. Flutes were also popular among Indians in North and South America. Today, the flute is still used among many Native Americans such as the Cahuilla, the Andean, and the Lakota.

Western flute

Look at the pictures of the two flutes. How are these flutes the same? How are they different?

Native American flute

LISTENING **Powama** *Cahuilla Song*

The words of the Cahuilla song "Powama" are "powama powama yawe." This means "these feathers move when you dance." Listen to Ernest Siva, a member of the Cahuilla Nation, play "Powama."

in Flight

🎵 El condor pasa *Andean Song*
LISTENING

The Indians of South America also have flute songs about birds. "El condor pasa" is a popular folk song which describes the majesty of the condor as it flies over the Andes mountains.

Edgar Zurita playing the quena.

Among many Native Americans, the flute was the instrument that a young man used to court a young woman. Each day, he played beautiful melodies for her. According to Lakota legend, the first flute was created to win the heart of an important chieftain's daughter. Here is the story:

During a time when food was difficult to find, a young man from a certain village goes hunting. As he is walking, he spots some elk tracks. He begins to follow the tracks and soon loses his way in the forest. Because it is too dark to return home, he decides to spend the night there. He begins to make his bed for the night, but he is stopped by a strange sound. He listens more closely. After a time, he falls asleep. He dreams. In his dream, he meets a red-headed woodpecker, "woknooka."

The next morning, the young man wakes up to the sight of the woodpecker sitting in a tree. As the bird flies from tree to tree, the young man follows him. Finally, the bird lands on a hollow branch. The wind blows through the branch. Suddenly, the young man remembers the sound of the wind blowing through the branch as the strange sound he heard the night before. He takes the branch and returns to his home.

Once he is back, he tries to make the beautiful sound he remembers. Nothing happens. After many failures, he goes back out to the forest by himself. Once again, he falls asleep. In his dream, the woodpecker reappears as a man who shows him how to make a flute from the hollow branch. When the young man wakes up, he goes home. Once there, he makes a flute. When he learns about the chieftain's daughter who will not fall in love with anyone, he decides that he will win her heart by making up special flute songs for her.

 LISTEN to Gary Fields, a member of the Lakota and Cree Nations, tell the story about the first flute.

This poem expresses the importance of flutes in Native American cultures.

FOR THE FLUTE PLAYERS

Theirs is the sound of wood
whispering Creator's breath
through branches hollowed
with sacred instruction

Theirs is the sound of breezes
dancing timeless songs
of passionate hearts
in circles around the Earth

Theirs is the sound of birds
sending meadow voices
on feathered wings
to all directions

Theirs is the sound of echoes
shaping red rock walls
in long canyon spaces
that remember forever

— Edwin Schupman
Muscogee (Creek)

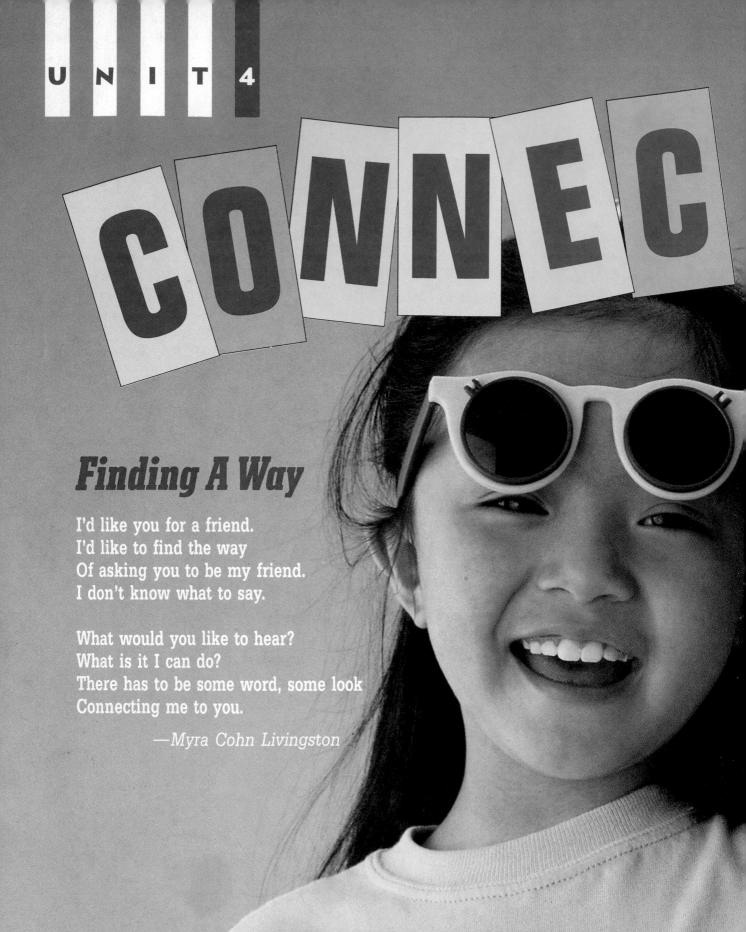

CONNEC

Finding A Way

I'd like you for a friend.
I'd like to find the way
Of asking you to be my friend.
I don't know what to say.

What would you like to hear?
What is it I can do?
There has to be some word, some look
Connecting me to you.

—Myra Cohn Livingston

TIONS

RHYTHM ALL AROUND

This song from southern Africa is about letting fire burn the bush, or wilderness area. Fire naturally clears the land of old shrub and allows space and sunlight for new growth. *Watsha* means "burn," and the song says "We are the burning fire; we burn, we burn."

SING this call-and-response song and pat with the beat.

Tina Singu

Song from Lesotho
As Sung by Kathleen Hill

Call   *Response*

Sotho: **Ti - na sing - u le - lu - vu - tae - o. Wat - sha, wat - sha, wat - sha,**
Pronunciation: ti na sing u lɛ lu vu tae o wat sha wat sha wat sha

Call   *Response*

Ti - na, Ti - na sing - u le - lu - vu - tae - o.
ti na ti na sing u lɛ lu vu tae o

1. **Wat - sha, wat - sha, wat - sha.**
wat sha wat sha wat sha

2. *Part 2* **wat - sha, la la la la la**
wat sha la la la la la

"Stone Pounding" was sung years ago by road workers, mostly women, as they broke large stones into smaller pieces. Now children play a game as they sing this song.

SWITCH between clapping the rhythm of the words and patting with the beat.

STONE POUNDING

Jamaican Folk Song
Transcribed by Helen H. Roberts

Three stone a stone, then a three stone a stone, then a

three stone a stone say tam-boo-lay and no quar-rel. You no

hear-e what me yer-ry? You no hear-e what me yer-ry? You no

hear-e what me hear, say tam-boo-lay and no quar-rel.

A D
Three stone a stone, then a three stone a stone, then a

D G D A7 D
three stone a stone, say tam-boo-lay and no quar-rel.

A NEW RHYTHM

The *short long short* pattern of sounds at the beginning of "Stone Pounding" lasts for two beats.

three   stone   a

Find two *short long short* patterns in the following phrase. Then clap the rhythm.

When *do* is D, as in "Stone Pounding," the key signature shows two **sharps** (♯). They tell you to play F sharp (F♯) and C sharp (C♯) instead of F and C.

These scenes show the festive costumes and traditional instruments of Andean carnivals. A Peruvian man plays a large flute (middle right) and the Bolivian marchers (middle left) play panpipes and drums. Bolivian and Peruvian musicians (opposite page) show two types of Andean flutes called quenas.

Guadalquivir *Andean Dance Song*

 LISTEN to "Guadalquivir" and raise your hand each time you hear the phrase with the *short long short* pattern. How many times do you hear the phrase?

"Guadalquivir" is a carnavalito. Carnavalitos blend South American Indian and Spanish musical traditions. They are usually sung and danced during festivals called carnivals.

Village carnivals may celebrate weddings, holy days, or anniversaries special to the village. People wear masks and fancy costumes, and enjoy singing, dancing, feasting, and parades.

PERFORM this step with the A section of "Guadalquivir."

right   left   right left   right   left   right   left   right left

LEAPIN'

Calypso is lively, rhythmic music of the West Indies.

SING the A section. Trace the melodic shape in the air and find the widest skips.

Hosanna, Me Build a House

Jamaican Calypso

Ho - san - na, me build a house, oh, ——

Ho - san - na, me build a house, oh, ——

1. I built it on the sand - y ground. ——
2. I built it on the sol - id ground. ——

Me house built on the sand - y ground. — It will fall you see.
Me house built on the sol - id ground. — It will stand you see.

Me house built on the sand - y ground. — It will fall you see.
Me house built on the sol - id ground. — It will stand you see.

C G7 C G7

The rain_____ will_____ wet_____ it up, ha! ha!
The rain_____ can't_____ wet_____ it up, ha! ha!

G7 C

The sun_____ will_____ burn_____ it up, ha! ha!
The sun_____ can't_____ burn_____ it up, ha! ha!

G7 C G7

The breeze_____ will_____ shake_____ it up, ha! ha!
The breeze_____ can't_____ shake_____ it up, ha! ha!

Da Capo after Verse 1
Coda after Verse 2

G7 C

The storm will bring it to the ground, ha! ha!
The storm can't bring it to the ground, ha! ha!

Coda *Sing 3 times*

G7 C F G7 C

Ho - san-na, me build a house, oh,— Ho - san-na!

THE OCTAVE: SOUND AND MOTION

Without motion, there can be no sound. When a drummer strikes a drum, a wind player blows on a reed, or a singer sings, an instrument is set in motion. The instrument sets the air in it and around it in motion. The motions that create sound are called **vibrations.** The higher a pitch is, the faster the vibrations.

An **octave** is a wide skip between two pitches. The higher pitch results from vibrations that are twice as fast as those that produce the lower pitch.

In this folk song, nonsense words called **vocables** are used to imitate the sound of a spinning wheel.

RAISE your hand when you hear an octave.

Dutch Spinning Song

Sa - ra - spon - da, Sa - ra - spon - da, Sa - ra - spon - da, Ret - set - set!

Sa - ra - spon - da, Sa - ra - spon - da, Sa - ra - spon - da, Ret - set - set!

Ah - do - ray - oh! Ah - do - ray - boom - day - oh!

Ah - do - ray - boom - day, Ret - set - set! Ah - say - pa - say - oh!

CULTURAL

Spirituals were created by African Americans, who combined African rhythms with melodies they created and heard in America. Many spirituals, such as this one about David and Goliath, are based on Biblical stories.

LITTLE DAVID, PLAY ON YOUR HARP

African American Spiritual

Refrain

Lit-tle Da-vid, play on your harp, Hal-le-lu! Hal-le-lu!

Lit-tle Da-vid, play on your harp, Hal-le-lu!_____

End (Fine)

Verse

1. Lit-tle Da-vid was a shep-herd boy, He
2. Old___ Da-vid was a might-y king, and

Go back to the beginning and sing to the end (Da Capo al Fine)

slew Go-li-ath and shout-ed for joy._____
all the peo-ple came___ to sing._____

144

CONNECTIONS

The stone carving (left) shows a woman playing a harp. The statue comes from Ur, a city of Sumeria, Mesopotamia, about 2,000 B.C. Above are designs from buildings of other Near Eastern civilizations that existed in Biblical times.

How high and low can you sing? The larynx, or voice box, is the part of your throat that vibrates as you make sound. The muscles of the larynx can tighten or loosen to produce a wide variety of pitches and qualities.

As a boy matures, his voice changes. His larynx gradually doubles in size, and the pitch of his voice becomes about an octave lower than it was. A girl's voice changes, too. Her larynx changes in texture rather than size, so the quality of her voice changes more than the pitch does.

MEET JOSEPH SHABALALA

Have you ever dreamed of taking your own special music to friends, neighbors, and beyond to the far corners of the earth? This is what Joseph Shabalala, founder of Ladysmith Black Mambazo, did. Starting with his own relatives, he developed a group that shares the musical traditions of the Zulu with people all over the world.

LISTEN to Joseph Shabalala talk about his career as a composer and leader of a musical group.

CONNECTING CULTURES

Many of the songs you sang in this unit were created by
people of African origin. Some of the people live there now.
Others have ancestors who came from Africa.

THINK IT THROUGH

Compare the rhythms, melodies, and ideas expressed in
the songs you sang. Find similarities and differences.

Drums play an important part in the music of Africa, including Zaire (top).
In Haiti, people of African descent carry on the tradition of drumming (left),
and in the United States, Chick Webb, an African American drummer, put
together the first standard trap set (right).

COME TO

Join the festive dancing! You've danced to the A section of "Guadalquivir." Here's the formation for the B section.

DANCE to "Guadalquivir."

CARNIVAL!

CONNECTING SOUND AND SYMBOL

The *short long short* pattern can be heard in both "Guadalquivir" and "Stone Pounding."

PAT and clap these two patterns from "Stone Pounding." How are they alike? How are they different?

Pat:

hear - e   what me

Clap:

three stone   a

Hear-e what me can be written this way.

Three stone a can be written two ways. A **tie** connects the two eighth notes that sound as one quarter note.

or

FIND this rhythm pattern in the music for "Stone Pounding" on page 136.

CARRY ON THE CARNIVAL RHYTHM

The ♪♩ ♪ rhythm can be found in the music of many parts of the world. In Egypt, you might hear this pattern played on a clay or metal hand drum called a dumbek.

PERFORM the pattern below as if you were playing a dumbek. Use one palm on *dum* and the fingertips of the other hand on *tak*. Say the words as you drum.

dum tak   tak dum   tak

LISTENING

Ayazein *Egyptian Folk Song*

LISTEN for the dumbek pattern in "Ayazein." Try to play along as you listen again!

Dumbeks are widely used in Middle Eastern countries, Turkey, and Greece. A floral pattern has been hammered into this metal dumbek from Turkey.

The dumbek is often played with other instruments. In this scene from Egypt, it is played with two rababas.

Which part of "Sarasponda" is this? Sing it with the "spinning words."

An octave is two pitches separated by a wide skip, with the higher pitch vibrating twice as fast as the lower. The two pitches have the same name. If C is the letter name of the lower pitch, what is the letter name of the higher pitch?

If *do* is the pitch syllable name of the lower pitch, what name is used for the pitch one octave higher?

CREATE a melodic ostinato using low and high *do*. Use the resonator bells C and C' and this rhythm pattern. Perform the ostinato with the A section of "Sarasponda."

Keep the ped - al mov - ing.   Keep the wheel a - turn - ing.

ANNA CODDE

Maerten van Heemskerck's portrait shows
a woman with her spinning wheel. The glowing
light and calm domestic scene are typical of Dutch
paintings from the 1500s. Imagine the turning
posts, spools, and wheel making rhythmic
sounds such as *ret set set* as they
spin fleece into wool.

LISTENING

Hoedown (excerpt) from *Rodeo*
by Aaron Copland

"Hoedown" borrows musical ideas from square dances and rodeos.

SING this motive with pitch syllables. Stamp on low *do* and clap on high *do*.

LISTENING MAP   Listen to "Hoedown" and follow the map.

KEY
a
b

A

START   a a b b a a b b b b a a   bridge
22 beats

B

16 beats

SPOTLIGHT ON AARON COPLAND

Aaron Copland (1900–1990) was born in Brooklyn, N.Y. His first contact with music came from listening to his older sister practice the piano. By age 8, he was composing songs. As an adult, he became one of the first American composers to have his work known all over the world.

Copland's use of jazz and American folk tunes gave his music a sound all its own. Besides composing for concerts, the ballet, opera, radio, theater, and movies, he was a pianist and conductor. He also lectured and wrote books to help people understand and appreciate modern music.

Voices in Harmony

When you sing or play pitches to accompany a melody, you produce harmony. By playing three or more pitches at the same time, you produce a **chord.** When the chord pitches change, the harmony of the song changes.

The harmony of "Hoe Ana Te Vaka" has changing chords.

RAISE your hand each time you hear a chord change. **Which instrument is playing the chords?**

In the South Pacific, the canoe has long been an important form of transportation. "Hoe Ana Te Vaka" describes paddling a canoe and sighting the islands of Tahiti and Mo'orea.

Hoe Ana Te Vaka

PADDLE THE CANOE

Tahitian Folk Song
Collected and Transcribed
by Kathy B. Sorensen

NAME THAT CHORD!

Each chord has a letter name based on a pitch called the **chord root.** Usually when the pitches of a chord are arranged close to each other on the staff, the lowest pitch is the chord root and gives the chord its name.

root   root   root

FIND the chord names above the music.

Me   house built_ on_ the sand-y ground._   It will fall you   see.

Me house built_ on_ the sand- y ground._   It will fall you   see.

HOSANNA!
WE BUILD A CHORD!

The colors show the harmonic pattern for the B section of "Hosanna, Me Build a House."

PLAY the harmonic pattern for "Hosanna, Me Build a House" with these three chords.

C E G F A C G B D

Rap and

Nathaniel Talking is a book of poetry by Eloise Greenfield. In the book, Nathaniel B. Free is a nine-year-old boy, and this is his rap.

Nathaniel's RAP

It's Nathaniel talking
and Nathaniel's me
I'm talking about
My philosophy
About the things I do
And the people I see
All told in the words
Of Nathaniel B. Free
That's me
And I can rap
I can rap
I can rap, rap, rap
Till your earflaps flap
I can talk that talk
Till you go for a walk
I can run it on down
Till you get out of town
I can rap
I can rap
Rested, dressed and feeling fine
I've got something on my mind

Rhythm

Friends and kin and neighborhood
Listen now and listen good
Nathaniel's talking
Nathaniel B. Free
Talking about
My philosophy
Been thinking all day
I got a lot to say
Gotta run it on down
Nathaniel's way
Okay!
I gotta rap
Gotta rap
Gotta rap, rap, rap
Till your earflaps flap
Gotta talk that talk
Till you go for a walk
Gotta run it on down
Till you get out of town
Gotta rap
Gotta rap
Rested, dressed and feeling fine
I've got something on my mind
Friends and kin and neighborhood
Listen now and listen good
I'm gonna rap, hey!
Gonna rap, hey!
I'm gonna rap!

—Eloise Greenfield

What can you tell about Nathaniel from
this poem?

**DESCRIBE how the poem could sound
when it is performed aloud as a rap.**

I Missed the Bus *by Jermaine Dupri*

In 1992 the rap duo Kris Kross recorded "I Missed the Bus."
They were 13 years old. Their special style is wearing every-
thing—hat, shirt, and jeans—backwards. But their music,
with its fresh rhythms and appealing rhymes, is what made
them successful. They've had a triple-platinum album,
Totally Krossed Out, from which "I Missed the Bus" is taken.

Rap sprang up in African American communities during
the 1970s. Rappers put together fast, catchy phrases over
rhythm tracks. Some rap is pure entertainment. Other
rappers' words turn to serious themes such as politics,
poverty, and racism.

LISTEN to "I Missed the Bus" and describe
what you hear.

Chris Smith
and Chris Kelly
of Kris Kross

In some music, stressed or **accented** sounds come between the beats instead of on the beat. Rhythm patterns with sounds between the beats are called **syncopated.**

Syncopation can be found in many kinds of music. The *short long short* pattern in "Stone Pounding" is an example of syncopation. The rhythms of rap are also very syncopated.

CREATE your own syncopated rap version of "Nathaniel's Rap."

THINK IT THROUGH

How would "Nathaniel's Rap" sound if every syllable were unaccented and on the beat? Try saying it that way. How does it compare with the recording?

MAKE YOUR OWN MELODY

Steel drums are tuned instruments made from oil drums and steel barrels. One drum can play up to thirty pitches, so a steel drum band can play both melody and harmony.

Steel drums accompany parades during Carnival. Steel drum bands, also called pan orchestras, are popular throughout the Caribbean and in other places with large numbers of West Indian people.

LISTEN to "Hosanna, Me Build a House" with steel drums playing the melody. When do the musicians make up new melodies in place of the melody of the song?

Steel drum band playing during Carnival in St. George's, Grenada. Opposite page: musicians playing steel drums on St. Lucia, a Caribbean island.

ADD SOME HIGHLIGHTS

Another way to change "Hosanna, Me Build a House" is to highlight parts of the melody by playing them on instruments. Find the pitches needed to play the tinted motives.

Ho - san - na, me build a house, oh, ____

Ho - san - na, me build a house, oh, ____

I built it on the sand - y ground. ____

PLAY the motives as you sing the song.

C D E F G A B C

What is the skip between the lowest and highest pitches called?

THE JAZZ CONNECTION

The syncopated rhythms and melodies of **jazz** grew from the spirituals, work songs, and blues of African Americans. The roots of jazz go back to rhythms from western Africa, which African Americans mixed with harmony from classical and folk music they learned in America. Jazz appeals to people of all cultures and many play this music.

Many jazz musicians are known for their ability to **improvise,** or find new ways to play melodies and rhythm patterns each time they perform.

meet
MARIAN McPARTLAND

Marian McPartland is a pianist and a songwriter who also improvises on other compositions, interpreting them her own way. She hosts a radio show, "Piano Jazz," on which she talks to and performs with other jazz pianists.

LISTEN to Marian McPartland as she discusses and demonstrates jazz improvisation.

LISTENING

Things Ain't What They Used to Be

by Mercer Ellington

LISTEN to Marian McPartland improvise on this jazz melody.

IMPROVISE melodies on these pitches during the verses of "Little David, Play on Your Harp."

Making Connections

When you meet someone new, you may first notice how that person is different from you. When you find something that is the same between you, such as an activity that you both enjoy, you have made a connection. You are on your way to being friends.

People everywhere enjoy playing together. "Stone Pounding" is a singing game from Jamaica.

Singing while you work can make the job easier. "Sarasponda" is a work song from Holland, and "Tina Singu" is one from Lesotho.

What other singing games do you know? What other work songs do you know?

CHECK IT OUT

1. How many times do you hear the *short long short* rhythm (♪ ♩ ♪) ?

    a. two times   **b.** three times   **c.** four times

2. Which rhythm do you hear?

a.

b.

c.

d.

3. Which pitches do you hear?

a.   C   **c.**   C

b.   C   **d.**   C

4. Which pitches do you hear?

a.   E   **c.**   E

b.   E   **d.**   E

CREATE

Syncopation in C

CREATE a melody using the pitches C D E G C^1. Use this rhythm pattern.

Write your melody on a staff. Where does it move by steps? by skips? Mark the steps with 1 and the skips with 2.

C is *do*. Sing your pattern with pitch syllable names.

PLAY your melody as an introduction to "Sarasponda."

Write

Explore your connections to the musical experiences of your family or neighbors.

Interview an older person to find out about his or her musical experiences. Ask about the person's favorite songs from school, or the musicians and groups that he or she enjoyed. Write a newspaper article about what you learn.

ENCORE

improvise!

Jazz musicians have always enjoyed the freedom of improvising. This allows them to change a piece of music as they play. Performing in this way did not start with jazz musicians. Performers have always improvised. Classical musicians such as Bach, Mozart, and Beethoven were masters of improvising at the keyboard.

SPOTLIGHT ON

CHARLIE PARKER

Charlie Parker, one of the all-time great saxophone players, was famous for his improvisations. Born in Kansas City in 1920, he began playing the alto saxophone when he was thirteen years old. During the 1940s, Parker's way of playing changed the style of jazz. His free style earned Parker the nickname "Bird."

The Charlie Parker combo in 1947, with Miles Davis playing trumpet.

LISTENING

Now's the Time (Versions 1 and 2)
by Charlie Parker

Listen to a twelve-bar blues piece composed by Charlie Parker. You will hear two versions. The first version was made for Bird, a movie about Charlie Parker. Using an old recording, engineers erased the drum, bass, and piano parts. Only the saxophone parts played by Charlie Parker were kept. New musicians were hired to play the other parts. The second version is the original recording of "Now's the Time."

DESCRIBE the differences you hear between the two recordings.

Sonny Rollins is a famous jazz saxophonist who, at one time, performed with Charlie Parker. Rollins, who was born in New York in 1930, made his most important contributions to jazz in the 1950s. His improvisations and his playing style were greatly admired.

LISTENING

Brilliant Corners

by Thelonious Monk

In "Brilliant Corners," Sonny Rollins performs with Thelonious Monk, pianist, and Max Roach, percussionist. They improvise question and answer phrases of different lengths.

LISTEN to this improvisation. How is this music like a conversation?

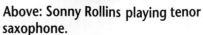

Above: Sonny Rollins playing tenor saxophone.
At left: Thelonious Monk at the piano.

Other artists also improvise in the way they use materials. Irene Bankhead, a quiltmaker, sews together beautiful pieces of cloth to make colorful designs. Bankhead, who started quilting when she was thirteen, can often finish a quilt in three days.

String **by Irene Bankhead**

Music with

a Message

PROVERBS BY AESOP

Slow and steady wins the race.
— *The Hare and the Tortoise*

**Don't count your chickens
before they are hatched.**
— *The Milkmaid and Her Pail*

Appearances are often deceiving.
— *The Wolf in Sheep's Clothing*

**No act of kindness, however small,
is wasted.**
— *The Lion and the Mouse*

Some Good

Here is an African song with a message: "Take time in life 'cause you got far way to go." What do you think this means?

TAKE TIME IN LIFE

Liberian Folk Song

1. I was pass - ing by, My broth - er called me in,
2. I was pass - ing by, My un - cle called me in,
3. I was pass - ing by, Some peo - ple called me in,

And he said to me, You bet - ter take time in life.
And he said to me, My neph - ew, take time in life.
And they said to me, My young man, take time in life.

Peo - ple, take time in life, Peo - ple, take time in life,
Neph - ew, take time in life, Neph - ew, take time in life,
Young man, take time in life, Young man, take time in life,

Peo - ple,
Neph - ew, } take time in life 'cause you got far way to go.
Young man,

What is the meter of "Take Time in Life"? How can you tell?

CREATE a beat pattern with movement to show how many beats are in each set.

Advice

LISTENING

D'Hammerschmiedsgesellen

Bavarian Folk Dance

The name of this dance means "The Journeyman Blacksmith." A journeyman was a young man learning a trade. Blacksmiths made horseshoes and other metal objects.

Listen to "D'Hammerschmiedsgesellen" to find the meter. Which meter signature fits the music?

2
4

3
4

4
4

CREATE a movement pattern to show how many beats are in each set.

THE STORIES YOU TELL!

Calypso is the name of Jacques Cousteau's ship. Cousteau studies underwater and coastal life in the oceans around the world. John Denver wrote this song to honor Cousteau's work.

Calypso

Words and Music
by John Denver

Freely

1. To sail on a dream on a crys-tal clear o-cean,
(2.) work in the ser-vice of life and the liv-ing,
(3.) part of the move-ment and part of the grow-ing,

To ride on the crest of the wild rag-ing storm.
In search of the an-swers to ques-tions un-known.
Part of be-gin-ning to un-der-stand.

2. To
3. To be

Aye,_____ Ca - lyp - so, the plac - es you've been to, The
Aye,_____ Ca - lyp - so, I sing to your spir - it, To

things that you've shown us, the sto - ries you tell! well. Hi - dee -
those who have served you so long and so

ay ee oo_____ oh - dle - oh oo_____ Hi - dee - oo_____

Which meter signature goes at the beginning of
"Calypso"? $\frac{2}{4}$ $\frac{3}{4}$ $\frac{4}{4}$

What riddles do you know? Riddles make you think about things in new ways. Find the riddles in "Tum-Balalaika."

Tum-Balalaika

Russian Yiddish Folk Song

Verse

Dm   A7

1. Maid - en, maid - en, can you ex - plain,
2. Fool - ish boy, I can ex - plain, A

A7   Dm

What can grow with - out an - y rain?
stone can grow with - out an - y rain.

Dm

What can burn for man - y a year?
True love can burn for man - y a year. A

C   A7   Dm

What can cry, and shed not a tear?
sad heart can cry, and shed not a tear.

THINKING

Refrain

Tum - ba - la, Tum - ba - la, Tum - ba - la - lai - ka,
tum ba la tum ba la tum ba la lai ka

Tum - ba - la, Tum - ba - la, Tum - ba - la - lai - ka,
tum ba la tum ba la tum ba la lai ka

Tum - ba - la - lai - ka, Tum - ba - la - lai - ka,
tum ba la lai ka tum ba la lai ka

Tum - ba - la - lai - ka, Tum - ba - la, tum!
tum ba la lai ka tum ba la tum

The balalaika is a popular Russian instrument that is played by rapidly plucking its three strings. Balalaikas of different sizes are played together in balalaika orchestras.

COUNTING IN MAORI

Children everywhere sing alphabet and counting songs. In New Zealand, Maori children count with this chant. Try counting from one to ten in Maori.

HEI TAMA TU TAMA

Sing three times counting 1 - 9

Traditional Maori Children's Counting Game

Maori: **Ka ta - hi, Hei ta - ma tu ta - ma**
Pronunciation: ka ta hi hei ta ma tu ta ma

Ka ru - a, Hei ta - ma tu ta - ma
ka ru a hei ta ma tu ta ma

Start here 4th time to count 10

Ka to - ru, Hei ta - ma tu ta - ma,
ka to ru hei ta ma tu ta ma

After 3rd time go to

Hei ta - ma tu ta - ma, Hei ta - ma tu ta - ma.
hei ta ma tu ta ma hei ta ma tu ta ma

Tahi, rua, toru are the words for "one, two, three."

Wha, rima, ono are "four, five, six."

Whitu, waru, iwa are "seven, eight, nine."

Tekau is "ten" and *tama* means "young boy."

184 SONGS FOR THINKING

MAJOR AND MINOR

The melodies of "Tum-Balalaika" and "Hei Tama Tu Tama" have different sounds. One reason is that they use different sets of pitches. The set of pitches heard in "Tum-Balalaika" is called **minor**. The set of pitches in "Hei Tama Tu Tama" is called **major**.

Tempo Terms

Folk dancers dance to both slow and lively music. Sometimes the music changes speed, challenging the dancers to go slower or faster.

clap

cross

legs

DANCE to "D'Hammer-schmiedsgesellen," a folk dance from the Bavarian region of Germany.

right

left

both

SPEED LIMIT AHEAD!

The **tempo** is the speed of the beat of a song. Here are some Italian words used to describe the tempo of music.

adagio	slow
moderato	medium
allegro	fast
presto	very fast

Music can begin at any tempo and then change. When the music speeds up, the change is called an **accelerando**, and when it slows down, the change is called a **ritardando**. Tempo changes can take you by surprise and make the music more interesting or expressive.

LISTEN for the tempos in "D'Hammerschmiedsgesellen."

Presto (excerpt) from Trio for Piano, Oboe, and Bassoon
by Francis Poulenc

The bassoon *and the* oboe *are woodwind instruments in the orchestra. If the bassoon's wooden tube were straightened out, it would measure $8\frac{1}{2}$ feet long! Because it is so long, the bassoon can play very low pitches. The player blows air through a* double reed, *two pieces of bamboo that are tied together and connected to the bassoon. The oboe is about 22 inches long and has a smaller double reed, producing higher, sweeter sounds. These two instruments are the main members of the double-reed branch of the woodwind family.*

oboe reed

bassoon reed

TIME FOR TI!

Listen as you sing the last phrase from "Hei Tama Tu Tama." You only sing *do* and a lower pitch. That pitch, just below *do*, is called *ti*.

The letter name for *do* in "Hei Tama Tu Tama" is F. What is the letter name for *ti*?

PLAY this phrase on an instrument.

Hei ta - ma tu ta - ma, Hei ta - ma tu ta - ma,

Hei ta - ma tu ta - ma._____

NAME the pitch syllables in this pattern.
Clue: The pattern ends on high *do* (*do'*).

do'

Raise your hand when you hear the pattern in "Aquaqua."

Aquaqua

Israeli Children's Game
Collected by Rita Klinger

Nonsense: A - qua qua del - la o - mar qua qua qua
Pronunciation: a kwa kwa de la o maɾ kwa kwa kwa

del si - ma tri - co tri - co tri - co tra
del si ma tri ko tri ko tri ko tra

va - lo va-lo va - lo va-lo va-lo va - lo 1 2 3 4 5
va lo va lo va lo va lo va lo va lo

In "Hei Tama Tu Tama," *do* is F. The key signature has a flat
(♭) on the third line. In "Aquaqua," *do* is C. How does its
key signature differ from the one in "Hei Tama Tu Tama"?

Look at the song again. A silence the length of an eighth
note is shown with an **eighth rest** (𝄾).

THE MAJOR SCALE

If you sing all the pitches from *do* to *do'*, you will be singing a **major scale**.

The C major scale looks like this.

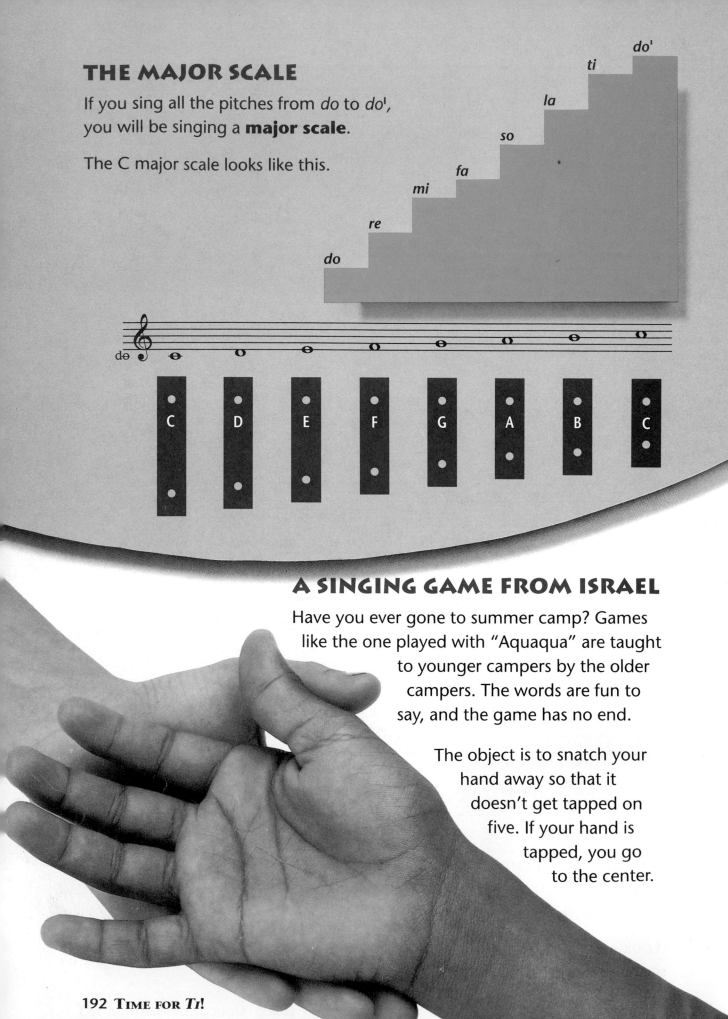

do *re* *mi* *fa* *so* *la* *ti* *do'*

C D E F G A B C

A SINGING GAME FROM ISRAEL

Have you ever gone to summer camp? Games like the one played with "Aquaqua" are taught to younger campers by the older campers. The words are fun to say, and the game has no end.

The object is to snatch your hand away so that it doesn't get tapped on five. If your hand is tapped, you go to the center.

Count out and tap hands.

Continue to five.

Music That

Music can carry a personal message, and it can also pass on the knowledge and traditions of a group of people.

LISTENING

Canoe Song and Dance

As Performed by Members of the Haliwa-Saponi Nation

Throughout their history, Native Americans have used songs and dances to teach life skills, such as hunting, and to tell stories. This Eastern Woodlands social dance tells the following story.

The women of the village are paddling canoes down the river to do the washing. They see the men of the village paddling upstream. The men are tired from the hard work of hunting. At first the men pass the women, but they are so happy to see each other that the men turn around and they all paddle downstream together.

Songs such as "Canoe Song and Dance" are learned by hearing someone sing them.

Eastern Woodlands canoe

Eastern Woodlands woven belt

Teaches Tradition

LEARN to sing "Canoe Song and Dance" by listening to these members of the Haliwa-Saponi Nation.

Canoe Dance performed by Haliwa-Saponi people of North Carolina.

TAKE TIME FOR A NEW RHYTHM

Which line shows the rhythm you performed with the first phrase of "Take Time in Life"?

The rhythm of the first phrase could be written like this.

SING the song on page 178 and find all the ♩. ♪ patterns.

A dot following a note adds half of the note's rhythmic value. A dot after a quarter note makes it an eighth note longer.

$$♪\_♪ = ♩$$

$$♪\_♪\_♪ = ♩.$$

$$♩\_♪ = ♩.$$

196

A RHYTHM RIDDLE

Which pattern below shows the correct notation for the first phrase of the refrain of "Tum-Balalaika"? For the first phrase of "Calypso"?

After you've solved the riddle, sing "Tum-Balalaika" with a soloist on each verse.

THINK IT THROUGH

How long would a dotted half note sound?
A dotted eighth note?

Dancing to Major and Minor

Most music is in either major or minor. Sometimes it's interesting to hear both in one piece.

SPOTLIGHT ON
Antonin Dvořák

Antonin Dvořák (1841–1904) was the son of a Czech innkeeper and butcher, who had hoped his son would stay in the business. Antonin played violin at the inn, and at 16 began to study music seriously. He learned to sing and to play violin, viola, organ, and piano. He later worked as a church organist and composer. Dvořák included Czech folk melodies in his pieces, and his tuneful, rhythmic music is still very popular.

LISTENING

Slavonic Dance Op. 46, No. 8

(excerpt)

by Antonin Dvořák

SIGNAL with your hand each time you hear a shift between minor and major.

What does the tempo marking tell you?

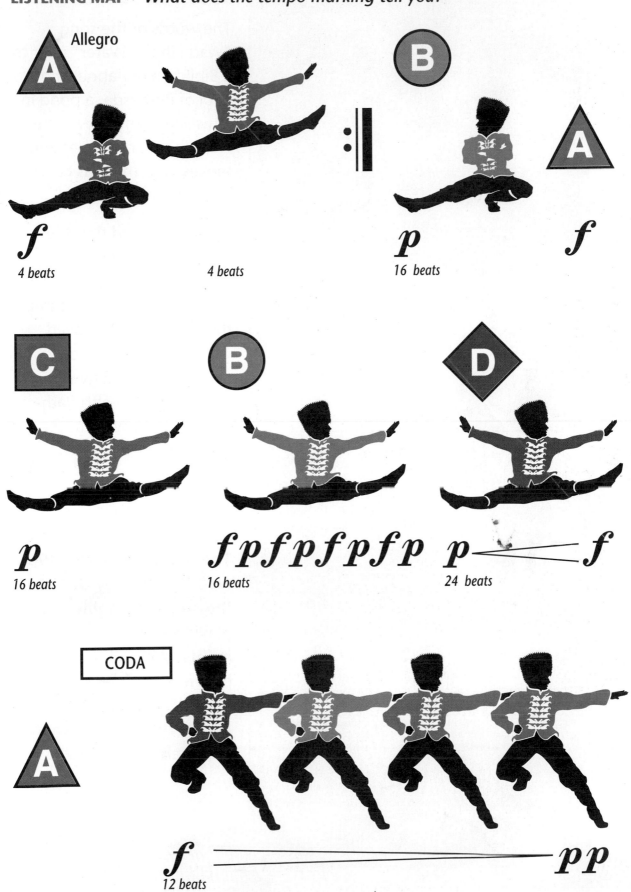

Allegro

A

f
4 beats

4 beats

B

A

p
16 beats

f

C
p
16 beats

B
fpfpfpfp
16 beats

D
p ◁ *f*
24 beats

CODA

A

f ———————— *pp*
12 beats

A SPIRITUAL

The words of the song "Wade in the Water" refer to a Biblical story about the Pool of Bethesda, a pond in Jerusalem. Sometimes the water's surface ripples and moves, and this was called "troubling the waters."

People believed that the pool was brushed by the wing of an angel, and that the first person to step into the water after it moved would be healed of diseases and ailments. Many who were in poor health gathered there to wait for the water to be "troubled."

DOWN BY THE RIVERSIDE

The musicians in this 1966 wood carving by Daniel Pressley are singing and playing traditional instruments, the guitar and the harmonica. The texture and depth of the carving add to the sense of energy and feeling in their music.

LISTEN to the song. Does it sound major or minor?

WADE IN THE WATER

Refrain

Group

African American Spiritual

Dm

Wade— in the wa-ter. Wade— in the wa-ter, chil-dren.

Dm

End (Fine)

Wade— in the wa-ter.— God's gon-na trou-ble the wa-ter.

Verse

Solo

Dm

Group

1. Tell you one thing and it's cer-tain-ly sure.
2. Who's that yon-der all— dressed— in white?
3. Who's that yon-der all— dressed— in red?
4. Up on the moun-tain Je - ho-vah, he spoke

Wade— in the wa-ter.—

Go back to the beginning and sing to the end (Da Capo al Fine)

Solo

Dm

Group

Judg-ment's com-in' and I don't— know.—
Looks like the chil-dren of the Is-rael-ites.—
Looks like the chil-dren that Mo-ses— led.—
Out of his mouth— came fire and— smoke.—

Wade— in the wa-ter.—

D·O·T·T·E·D
Rhythms Return

Name a song you know for each picture.

CLAP the rhythm and match it to a phrase from one of the songs.

Singing is an important part of German culture, and songs such as this canon are traditional favorites.

Find the rhythm that is always sung with the word *Musica*.

TAP or play this rhythm each time you sing it.

Music Alone Shall Live
Himmel und Erde

German Round
Words Adapted by MMH

German: Him - mel und Er - de müss - en ver - gehn;
Pronunciation: hɪ məl ʊnt ɛɹ də mö sən fɛɹ gen
English: All things will per - ish be - neath___ the sky;

a - ber die Mu - si - ca, a - ber die Mu - si - ca,
a bəɹ di mu zi kɑ a bəɹ di mu zi kɑ
Mu - sic a - lone shall live, Mu - sic a - lone shall live,

a - ber die Mu - si - ca blei - bet be - stehn.
a bəɹ di mu zi kɑ blaɪ bət bə shten
Mu - sic a - lone shall live, nev - er to die.

Galliard *by Tielman Susato*

The galliard, an athletic and energetic dance, was one of the most popular dances in European courts during the 1500s. It was the only court dance for which the men removed their hats—which otherwise would have fallen off!

CLAP the rhythm of the A section of "Galliard." Which part is the same as the rhythm of the words *aber die Musica*?

LISTEN to all of "Galliard" to hear how many times this rhythm is played in the melody:

Boy Playing Flute by Judith Leyster. Statens Konstmuseer, Stockholm, Sweden

BOY PLAYING FLUTE Judith Leyster painted this around 1630. The boy is playing a kind of flute which was played either to the right or to the left. On the wall are a Baroque violin and bow and a recorder.

WOODWINDS OF THE RENAISSANCE

In "Galliard" you hear several Renaissance woodwind instruments. Each section of the music is repeated. The first time through each section, the music is played on recorders.

When each section is repeated, you hear shawms and krummhorns. These are double-reed instruments that were early forms of the bassoon and oboe.

Recorders

Shawm

Krummhorn

A MAJOR

"Hei Tama Tu Tama" sounds major. What is its tonal center?

When a song has *do* as its tonal center, it is in major. "Hei Tama Tu Tama" is in F major. The pitches in this song come from the F major scale.

PLAY and sing a major scale, beginning on F.

do re mi fa so la ti do'

When F is *do*, there is a flat on the B line of the staff. This flat tells you to use B flat (B♭) instead of B in this song. Notice the black key (B♭) that is used in the F major scale.

EVENT

ADD MINOR HARMONY

When a song has *la* as its tonal center, it is in minor. "Wade in the Water" is in D minor. The pitches you sing come from the D **minor scale**.

la, ti, do re mi fa so la

A scale in D minor has the same key signature as one in F major. The scale in F major begins and ends on *do*. The scale in D minor begins and ends on *la*.

SING this harmony part with the refrain of **"Wade in the Water."**

Wade on chil-dren, wade— in the wa-ter. Wade, chil - dren,   Wade on.

PLAY a minor scale beginning on D. Remember to play a B♭.

Verse

Solo
Dm

Group

C   Dm

1. Tell you one   thing   and it's cer-tain-ly   sure.
2. Who's_ that   yon-der all_ dressed   in white?
3. Who's_ that   yon-der all_ dressed   in red?
4. Up   on the moun-tain Je - ho-vah, he spoke.

Wade_ in the wa-ter._

Go back to the beginning
and sing to the end
(Da Capo al Fine)

Solo
Dm

Group

C   Dm

Judg-ment's com-in'   and   I don't_ know._
Looks like the child-ren of the   Is-rael - ites._
Looks like the child-ren that Mo-ses_ led._
Out of   his   mouth_ came fire and_ smoke._

Wade_ in the wa-ter._

*Note: Cue notes may be sung or replaced with improvisation.

IMPROVISE and sing your own melodies with these pitches. They are the pitches of the harmony part.

Use resonator bells or a keyboard to help you.

D   E   F   G   A   C   D

REVIEW

SONGS THAT TEACH

Think of something you learned today and how you learned it. Share that information with your neighbor.

SING the song that goes with each picture. What can each song teach you?

Hei Tama Tu Tama

Tum-Balalaika

Which songs are in minor? Major?
Which songs are in $\frac{3}{4}$? $\frac{4}{4}$?

MAKE up your own question about one
of the songs to ask your neighbor.

Take Time in Life

CHECK IT OUT

1. Which example is in ⅜ ?

    a. Example 1   **b.** Example 2

2. Which example is in ¾ ?

    a. Example 1   **b.** Example 2

3. Which rhythm do you hear?

    a.

    b.

    c.

    d.

4. Which rhythm do you hear?

    a.

    b.

    c.

    d.

CREATE

Playing with Threes

CREATE an accompaniment of four measures for "Tum-Balalaika." Use these rhythm patterns.

EXPERIMENT with different combinations of the rhythm patterns. Play them on tambourines or other percussion instruments.

Which combination of rhythms do you like with the song? Why?

Write

Which message from the songs in this unit meant the most to you?

Write several sentences explaining the message and what it means to you.

Singing Reeds

Have you ever held two blades of grass together with your thumbs, and blown between them? You might have heard the same sound early musicians heard thousands of years ago when they tried this.

A double-reed instrument is a wind instrument with two blades, or reeds, that vibrate together when air passes between them. These reeds may be made of cane, metal, or even plastic.

The two double-reed instruments that are the most familiar to us today are the oboe, a higher-pitched instrument, and the bassoon, a larger, lower-pitched instrument.

Sounds of the Oboe

LISTEN to the sound of an oboe. How would you describe this sound?

Some form of the oboe has been popular since 3000 B.C. The oboe comes from the shawm, a simple pipe with a double reed. Shawms were played in India, China, Egypt, and Greece before they were brought to western Europe.

Playing the ancient oboe, or aulos, was one of the main athletic events in the original Olympic Games in Greece. The aulos was so difficult to blow that these players became real heroes. Often the sound of the aulos accompanied Roman gladiators as they fought in the arena, or soldiers as they marched into battle.

A Grecian cup, painted about 460 B.C. in the province of Attica, shows a young man playing an aulos.

The Nagasvaram shawm of India comes from an ancient Persian shawm. It has a loud tone which makes it a popular instrument in outdoor ceremonies.

LISTENING

Sounds of the Bassoon

One early name for the bassoon was dulcian. *Dulcian is from the Latin word* dulcis, *which means "soft" or "sweet." In the 1500s, the dulcian developed into the early bassoon.*

LISTEN to the bassoon. **Why do you think it is related to the dulcian?**

The oboe and bassoon have changed many times during the past three hundred years. Extra keys have been added to make them easier to play.

COMPARE the number of keys on each instrument below.

Baroque oboe

Modern oboe

Baroque bassoon

Modern bassoon

A WORLD

ROCKS

Big rocks into pebbles
Pebbles into sand.
I really hold a million million rocks here in my hand.

— *Florence Parry Heide*

OF CHANGE

MAKE A CHANGE

Who or what is changing in this song?
How will this change happen?

I Can Be

Words and Music by
Anthony Q. Richardson

Introduction

This is the day,— I will make a change,— all I have to do—

Sing bracketed section twice

Part 1 Make a change.——

Part 2 It's up to me.——

I can be what-

(mf on repeat)

ev - er I want to be. All I do is try a lit - tle

hard - er. I can do what - ev - er I want to do.

Repeat 1st time only

All I do is try a lit - tle hard - er.

All I have to do— is get an ed‑u‑ca‑tion,—

Repeat 2nd time only **D.S.** 𝄋

be what I want to be.— I can set my‑self free.—

Sing 1. and 2. three times
Beginning with lowest line, add a part on each repetition

Part 3

1. I can be what‑ev‑er I want to be.
2. I can do what‑ev‑er I want to do.

Parts 1 and 2

1. I can be what‑ev‑er I want to be.
2. I can do what‑ev‑er I want to do.

All I do is try a lit‑tle hard‑er.

All I do is try a lit‑tle hard‑er.

All I have to do— is get an ed - u - ca - tion,—

be what I want to be.— I can set my-self free.—

Coda

This is the day,——— I will make a change,— all I have to do—

Part 1 Make a change.————————————

Part 2 It's up to me.——

decresc.

This is the day,——— I will make a change,- all I have to do—

Part 1 Make a change.————————————

Parts 2 and 3 It's up to me.——

SING the first page with the dynamics as marked.

How do you think the change in dynamics brings out the meaning of the words?

CHOOSE dynamics that help to express the feelings in this song.

THIS PRETTY PLANET

Words and Music by
John Forster and Tom Chapin

This pret - ty plan - et spin - ning through space.— You're a

gar - den. You're a har - bor. You're a ho - ly place.— Gold - en

sun go - ing down.— Gen - tle blue gi - ant, spin us a - round.—

All through the night. Safe 'til the morn - ing light.—

 LISTENING # Korobushka *Russian Folk Song*

In Russia, a korobushka is a cart in which a peddler carries all sorts of items for sale.

LISTEN for musical changes in "Korobushka." Move to the music.

Read the lyrics. How would you change the accompaniment with each verse?

THE CAT CAME BACK

American
Folk Song
Arranged by
Mary Goetze

Verse *Freely*

1. Old Farm-er John-son had trou-bles all his own. He
2. Farm-er John-son's neigh-bor swore he'd chase him out of sight. He

had a lit-tle cat that would-n't leave his home. He
donned his fast-est shoes and he ran with all his might. The

tried and he tried to give that cat a-way! He
cat was quick, he ran a-way and John-son's neigh-bor fell.

Refrain

gave it to a man go-ing far, far a-way.— But the
Peo-ple came from miles a-way be-cause they heard him yell.— But the

Part 1

cat came back— the ver-y next day.— The

Part 2

cat came back! We thought he was a gon-er. The

COMPANIMENT

cat came back!— We thought he was a gon-er, but the

cat came back!— We thought he was a gon-er. The

cat came back,— He just would-n't stay a-way.—

cat came back,— He would-n't stay a-way.—

Interlude *(Sing after 1st, 2nd, and 4th Refrain)*

Part 1

Part 2

Du-du-du-doop! Me-ow!— Du-wa,— du-du-du-doop! Me-ow!—

Go to Coda after 4th Refrain **Coda**

Du-wa!— He just would-n't stay a-way. Du-du-du-doop! Yeah!

3. He gave it to a man
   going up in a balloon.
   Told him to give it
   to the man up in the moon.
   The balloon came down
   about ninety miles away.
   What happened to the man?
   I really couldn't say. *Refrain*

4. A great tornado came
   just the other day.
   The wind began to blow,
   the trees began to sway.
   Thunder struck, lightning flashed,
   darkness took the day.
   The people were so frightened,
   they knelt right down to pray. *Refrain*

A MUSICAL TALL TALE

"Old Joe Clark" is based on an old fiddle tune.
What does the song tell you about Old Joe?

Old Joe Clark

American Folk Song

Refrain

'Round and 'round, Old Joe Clark, 'Round and 'round I say;

'Round and 'round, Old Joe Clark, I have-n't long to stay.

Verse

1. Old Joe Clark, he had a house, six-teen sto-ries high.
2. I went down to Joe Clark's house, nev-er been be-fore.
3. Joe Clark had a vi-o-lin, he fid-dled all the day.

Go back to the beginning and sing to the end (Da Capo al Fine)

Ev'-ry sto-ry in that house was full of chick-en pie.
He slept on the feath-er bed and I slept on the floor.
An-y-bod-y start to dance and Joe would start to play.

Many people have enjoyed making up verses about Old Joe.

WRITE your own verse for this tall tale.

CREATE A RHYTHMIC ACCOMPANIMENT

Choose a word or idea from each verse. Create a four-beat rhythmic ostinato to accompany that verse. Here are some examples for the first verse.

Chick,   chick,   chick-en chick-en

How   high?——   Oh my!

Bring me   some pie.

PLAY an ostinato with each verse using different combinations of sounds.

CHANGING COLORS

Each instrument pictured here
has its own special sound, or tone color.
As you listen to "The Court of King Carraticus,"
each instrument's sound will cue you to move differently. The pictures show you the motions.

PLAY the sound cue game!

vibraslap   court

drum   faces

gong   palace

triangle   noses

claves   ladies

maracas   powder

**PERFORM the motion that goes
with each tone color as you hear it.**

The Court of King Carraticus

American
Nonsense Song

verses accumulate

1. Oh, the court of King Car-ra-ti-cus is just pass-ing by;
2. Oh, the pal-ace of the court of King Car-ra-ti-cus

Oh, the court of King Car-ra-ti-cus is just pass-ing by;
Oh, the pal-ace of the court of King Car-ra-ti-cus

Oh, the court of King Car-ra-ti-cus is just pass-ing by;
Oh, the pal-ace of the court of King Car-ra-ti-cus

Oh, the court of King Car-ra-ti-cus is just pass-ing by.
Oh, the pal-ace of the court of King Car-ra-ti-cus

Add one phrase on each repetition of the song.

3. ladies of the palace of the court of
   King Carraticus are just passing by.

4. faces of the...

5. noses of the...

6. powder on the...

7. If you want to take a photo of the...

(spoken at end)
It's too late! They just passed by!

A RAINBOW OF PERCUSSION INSTRUMENTS

This song teases Michie Banjo for his fancy clothes. Listen for the tone colors in the accompaniment of this song.

Michie Banjo

Creole Bamboula
English Words by
Margaret Marks

Refrain

Look at Mich-ie Ban-jo, Fan-cy Mich-ie Ban-jo,
mi shi

Strut-tin' down the street.

Verse

1. Cha-peau cocked on one side, Mich-ie Ban-jo,
   sha po
2. Dia-mond pin in his tie, Mich-ie Ban-jo,

High but-ton shoes that squeak.
Bright yel-low gloves so neat.

Walk-in' stick a-swing-in' wide, Mich-ie Ban-jo,
Trou-sers pleat-ed way up high, Mich-ie Ban-jo,

Go back to the beginning and sing to the end
(Da Capo al Fine)

Ev'-ry-thing's all com-plete.
Ev'-ry-thing's all com-plete.

The Orff instruments include large and small percussion instruments with bars of wood or metal. These bars are tuned to definite pitches. Orff instruments are often played with a variety of nonpitched percussion instruments. You hear them all together in "Michie Banjo."

bass xylophone

alto xylophone

soprano xylophone

alto metallophone

bass metallophone

soprano metallophone

soprano glockenspiel

alto glockenspiel

claves

tambourine

triangle

A MINOR CHANGE

meet Anthony Richardson

The composer of "I Can Be," Anthony Richardson, wrote this song for his music students at an elementary school in Memphis, Tennessee.

LISTEN as Anthony Richardson talks about why he wrote this song. Then sing "I Can Be" on page 220. Sing in three parts as shown in the score.

A sharp (♯), a flat (♭), or a **natural** (♮) sign that appears next to a pitch and is not in the key signature is called an **accidental.** The accidental changes how the pitch should be sung.

G♭ sounds a little lower than G.

G♯ sounds a little higher than G.

G♮ reminds you to sing G.

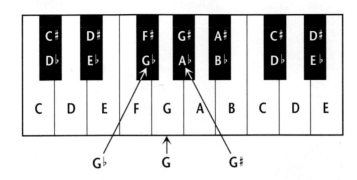

MAJOR OR MINOR?

Listen to a major scale beginning on E, then to a minor scale beginning on E.

SING each scale with the correct pitch syllables.

do re mi fa so la ti do'

E major scale

la, ti, do re mi fa so la

E minor scale

Look at "Korobushka" as you listen to it. Does its melody use the pitches of a major scale or a minor scale? How do you know?

SIMPLY BEAUTIFUL

The Shakers, a religious group, live a strict and simple life. They organize their time, tools, and homes carefully, wasting nothing.

SING "Simple Gifts," a well-known Shaker song.

This chair and lamp stand show the simple, graceful design typical of the Shakers, who make everything they use.

SIMPLE GIFTS

Shaker Song

'Tis the gift to be sim-ple, 'tis the gift to be free,

'Tis the gift to come down where we ought to be.

And when we find our-selves in the place just right,

'Twill be in the val-ley of love and de-light.

Refrain

When true sim-pli-ci-ty is gained,

To bow and to bend we shan't be a-shamed.

To turn, turn will be our de-light,

Till by turn-ing, turn-ing we come 'round right.

DOUBLE the Fun

FIND the connection between the two patterns on each line.

A **whole note** (○) shows a sound that lasts for four beats in 𝄴.

When you change a rhythm by making it twice as long, you **augment** it. To augment means to make larger. For example, when you augment a sound one beat long, it becomes a sound two beats long. In 𝄴, each quarter note will become a half note.

If you augment a rhythm in 𝄴, what would a half note become?

SAY this poem as you tap with the beat.

Clickbeetle

Click beetle
Clack beetle
Snapjack black beetle
Glint glitter glare beetle
Pin it in your hair beetle
Tack it to your shawl beetle
Wear it at the ball beetle
Shine shimmer spark beetle
Glisten in the dark beetle
Listen to it crack beetle
Click beetle
Clack beetle

—Mary Ann Hoberman

CHANGE the way you say the poem by augmenting the rhythm of the words as you tap the beat.

THINK IT THROUGH

How does augmenting the rhythm of the words change the way you imagine the clickbeetle?

LISTENING

Appalachian Spring (excerpt)
by Aaron Copland

The ballet Appalachian Spring *is about a pioneer couple's wedding day. Copland's music for the ballet includes the melody of "Simple Gifts." The melody is repeated and changed in a variety of ways. You will hear its rhythm augmented and also hear the melody played as a canon.*

OFF FRANKLIN OR NOLENSVILLE PIKE, NASHVILLE

Mayna Treanor Avent's painting shows the sunny rural beauty that may have inspired *Appalachian Spring.*

PAT with the beat and sing this phrase of "Simple Gifts."

'Tis the gift to be sim-ple, 'tis the gift to be free,

'Tis the gift to come down where we ought to be.

PAT with the beat and sing the same phrase, this time augmenting the rhythm.

'Tis the gift to be sim-ple, 'tis the gift to be free,

'Tis the gift to come down where we ought to be.

Listen for the augmentation of "Simple Gifts" in *Appalachian Spring.*

THE CLARINET

The **clarinet** is a woodwind instrument that comes in a variety of sizes. A musician blows on a single **reed,** a piece of cane attached to the mouthpiece, to make the air inside the instrument vibrate and produce sound. Listen as the clarinet begins the music from *Appalachian Spring.*

clarinet

single reed

CHANGING

Sing "This Pretty Planet." As you sing, pat with the beats that feel strongest and clap with the other beats. How are the beats grouped?

MOVE to "This Pretty Planet" in $\frac{4}{4}$.

1. Walk clockwise, then counterclockwise.

2. Face the center of the circle and raise your arms, then lower your arms.

METER

3. Turn in place.

4. Walk toward the center of the circle, then walk back out.

NEW PLANET

Changing the meter of a song gives a new feeling to the music. Here is "This Pretty Planet" in ⅜. Compare it with the same song in ¼ on page 223.

SING the song with two different meters.

This Pretty Planet

Words and Music by
John Forster and Tom Chapin
Adapted by MMH

This pret-ty plan-et spin-ning through space. You're a gar-den. You're a har-bor. You're a ho-ly place. Gold-en sun go-ing down. Gen-tle blue gi-ant, spin us a-round. All through the night. Safe 'til the morn-ing light.

THINK IT THROUGH

What happens to the sets of beats when the meter changes? Which meter do you prefer, and why?

Some songs stay in the same meter; others change meter.

PAT with the beats that feel strongest as you listen to "The Court of King Carraticus." What happens?

UNTITLED
Keith Haring's artwork expresses his wish for people to join together to enjoy and take care of the planet Earth.

PLAIN and FANCY

Compare each pair of objects. How are they different?

One of each pair is simple and the other is ornate, or decorated. Music can be ornate also. A song can be decorated by adding pitches to the melody. This is called **ornamentation.**

COMPARE the pictures in the frames below.

This shows the original melody of "Music Alone Shall Live."

Him - mel   und   Er -   de

müss - en   ver -   gehn;

Here is the same melody with three types of ornamentation.

trill   turn   slide

Him - mel   und   Er -   de   müss- en   ver-   gehn;

ORNAMENTS FROM AROUND THE WORLD

Vocal ornamentation is practiced by singers from all over the world. In some styles of music, the composer suggests how to ornament the melody. In others, the performers are creative in adding pitches to the song.

LISTENING

Vocal Ornamentation Montage

Listen to how these singers use ornamentation.

African American– turns, slides

Indian– trills, slides

Hopi–slide

Palestinian–trills, turns

FANCY THAT!

Here's the beginning of the refrain of "Old Joe Clark."

Old Joe Clark
'Round and 'round,

How would "Old Joe Clark" sound with ornamentation? Try these versions.

1. slide

Old Joe Clark
'Round and 'round,

2. trill

Old Joe Clark
'Round and 'round,

3. turn
Old Joe Clark
'Round and 'round,

CHOOSE the way you'd like to ornament "Old Joe Clark." Then sing the song and use your ornamentation at the beginning of the refrain.

Change= Variation

One of the many ways to change or vary a piece of music is to change the melody. A composer writes music based on a melody. Different treatments of that melody follow. The form of the music is called **theme and variations.** The original melody is the theme, and each changed version of the melody is called a variation. The theme sounds different in each variation, but you can still recognize it.

Look at these seven ways to vary a melody. Name the songs that were varied in these ways.

- dynamics
- tempo
- tone color
- rhythm
- meter
- pitch
- accompaniment

LISTENING

Variations on an American Theme

by Linda Worsley

LISTENING MAP *The theme, "The Battle Hymn of the Republic," is presented first, followed by the variations. Listen for all the ways the theme is varied.*

INTRODUCTION
AND THEME
All

VARIATION 1
LIVELY
Woodwinds

VARIATION 2
LYRICAL
Woodwinds

VARIATION 3
MARCHING
Brass

VARIATION 5
PLAYFUL
Unpitched Percussion

VARIATION 4
SINGING
Brass

VARIATION 6
MARCHING
Pitched Percussion

VARIATION 7
LYRICAL
Arco Strings

VARIATION 8
LIVELY
Pizzicato Strings

THEME
A SECTION
STATELY
All

THEME
B SECTION
STATELY
All

CODA
All

249

VARIATIONS ON "MUSIC ALONE SHALL LIVE"

Now it's your turn to be the composer!

CREATE a set of variations using "Music Alone Shall Live" as your theme. Divide into groups and choose one of these ideas to change the theme.

Rhythm and Meter

Change the meter from ¾ to ⁴⁄₄. For example, change the rhythm of the words *aber die Musica.*

a - ber die Mu - si - ca

Tone Color

Change the vocal tone color by whispering or speaking. Or play the song on percussion instruments.

Accompaniment

Decide whether to perform the song as a two- or three-part canon. Decide when each part will start.

Dynamics

Use any or all of these markings to change dynamics.

f, p, mf, mp, ,

Tempo

Decide which tempos and tempo changes to use.

adagio, moderato, allegro, presto, accelerando, ritardando

Pitch

You can slide, trill, or turn to ornament the melody.

PERFORM your variation as part of a class performance of "Variations on 'Music Alone Shall Live.'"

ALL KINDS OF CHANGES

Describe the musical changes you see. What other ways can you make changes?

Make some changes as you sing "Simple Gifts," "The Cat Came Back," and "I Can Be."

CHECK IT OUT

1. Listen to two examples. Is the second rhythm an augmentation of the first?

   a. Yes   **b.** No

2. Listen to two examples. Is the second rhythm an augmentation of the first?

   a. Yes   **b.** No

3. Which phrase is in minor?

   a. Phrase 1   **b.** Phrase 2   **c.** Phrase 3   **d.** Phrase 4

4. Listen to two examples. How do the dynamics and tempo change in the second example?

   a. faster and louder   **c.** slower and louder

   b. faster and softer   **d.** slower and softer

5. Listen to two examples. How does the accompaniment change in the second example?

   a. A rhythmic ostinato is added.

   b. A vocal melodic line is added.

   c. The melody is sung as a canon.

   d. There is no change.

CREATE

Melody in Minor

CREATE a melody for part of the poem "Clickbeetle."

Every time you and your partner have the word "beetle," play the pitch A. Choose the rest of your pitches from the minor scale that starts on A.

A   B   C   D   E   F   G   A

Write the pitch letter names you choose on a sheet of paper. Play your part in a performance of the whole poem.

Write

What do you like most about music class? What would you like most to change? What would you like to learn more about?

Write a letter to your teacher explaining your favorite and least favorite music class, and what musical activities you look forward to in the future.

ENCORE FOR THE RECORD

The Granger Collection

When Thomas Edison shouted "Mary had a little lamb" into the mouthpiece of his invention, in 1877, he recorded the first sounds on the first phonograph.

Edison's first "record" was a small metal cylinder. The recorded sound was very weak. After many improvements, people could listen to their favorite music on discs played on the gramophone.

By 1925, phonograph records were developed. Early records were large and easily broken. Each side held about six minutes of sound. By the late 1940s, long-playing records that held about thirty minutes of sound on each side began to replace the older records.

...or let 'em spin

The phonograph at left is a very early model. Radio/record players such as the one above were used for long-playing records.

STANDARD
MODEL A

By the 1950s, the sound quality of records was improved. Through stereophonic sound, two separate tracks of sound, one on the left and one on the right, give the impression of a live performance. When the two tracks are combined, the sound seems to surround the listener.

Left to right: records called 45s, a record player insert for playing 45s, jukebox, cassette tape, portable tape player, CDs.

At one time, music stores were filled with rows of record albums. But today, the racks are filled with tapes and CDs. Cassette tapes became popular when small tape recorders were developed. A tape player can be easily carried to the beach or park.

The CD, or compact disc, is much smaller than the record. The sound is very clear. There are no slight hissing noises which records sometimes pick up.

A CD player uses laser technology. When a laser beam passes over one side of the disc, it crosses many pits, which contain the information that will become the music you hear. Now, you can enjoy eighty minutes of music on one CD.

New types of CDs and tapes are still being developed. The CDs and tapes of the future will be even smaller and lighter than those popular today.

Live Aid concert, 1985, for African famine relief.

LIV AID

ations

FESTIVAL

First of all
Fast of all,
Feast of all—
Festival

—John Kitching

People play and sing the national anthem of their country on official occasions, at athletic events, and to honor the country's leader.

"The Star-Spangled Banner" is the national anthem of the United States. The words of the song recall an important event in the history of the country.

THE STAR-SPANGLED BANNER

Music Attributed to J. S. Smith
Words by Francis Scott Key

1. Oh, — say! can you see, by the dawn's ear - ly light,
2. On the shore, dim - ly seen through the mists of the deep,
3. Oh, — thus be it ev-er when — free men shall stand

What so proud - ly we hailed at the twi-light's last gleam-ing?
Where the foe's haugh - ty host in dread si - lence re - pos - es,
Be - tween their loved homes and the war's des - o - la - tion!

Katharine Lee Bates traveled across the United States about a hundred years ago. Her trip inspired the poem that became "America, the Beautiful." The words capture not only the beauty of the American landscape, but also the pride Bates felt for her country.

AMERICA,
the Beautiful

Music by Samuel Ward
Words by Katharine Lee Bates

1. O beau-ti-ful for spa-cious skies, For am-ber waves of grain.
2. O beau-ti-ful for pil-grim feet, Whose stern im-pas-sioned stress
3. O beau-ti-ful for he-roes proved In lib-er-at-ing strife,
4. O beau-ti-ful for pa-triot dream That sees be-yond the years,

For pur-ple moun-tain maj-es-ties a-bove the fruit-ed plain.
A thor-ough-fare for free-dom beat a-cross the wil-der-ness.
Who more than self their coun-try loved, and mer-cy more than life.
Thine al-a-bas-ter cit-ies gleam Un-dim'd by hu-man tears.

A - mer-i-ca! A - mer-i-ca! God shed His grace on thee,
A - mer-i-ca! A - mer-i-ca! God mend thine ev'-ry flaw,
A - mer-i-ca! A - mer-i-ca! May God thy gold re-fine,
A - mer-i-ca! A - mer-i-ca! God shed His grace on thee,

And crown thy good with broth-er-hood, From sea to shin-ing sea.
Con-firm thy soul in self-con-trol, Thy lib-er-ty in law.
Till all suc-cess be no-ble-ness, And ev'-ry gain di-vine.
And crown thy good with broth-er-hood, From sea to shin-ing sea.

Many people who live in the United States have come from other countries. The first line of "This Is My Country" has words for everyone who is happy to live in the United States of America.

This Is My Country

Music by Al Jacobs
Words by Don Raye

1.–2. This is my coun-try! Land of my { birth. choice.

This is my coun-try! { Grand-est on earth. Hear my proud voice.

I pledge thee my al-le-giance, A-mer-i-ca the bold, for

This is my coun-try, to have and to hold!

The words to "America" were first recited at a children's Fourth of July picnic in Boston in the 1800s. Later, Reverend Smith, the man who wrote the words, chose a hymnlike tune from a collection of German melodies to set the words to music.

AMERICA

Music by
Henry Carey
Words by
Samuel F. Smith

1. My coun-try, 'tis of thee, Sweet land of
2. My na-tive coun-try thee, Land of the
3. Let mu-sic swell the breeze, And ring from
4. Our fa-thers' God, to Thee, Au-thor of

lib - er - ty, Of thee I sing.
no - ble free, Thy name I love.
all the trees Sweet Free - dom's song;
lib - er - ty, To Thee we sing.

Land where my fa - thers died, Land of the Pil - grim's pride,
I love thy rocks and rills, Thy woods and tem - pled hills;
Let mor - tal tongues a - wake, Let all that breathe par - take,
Long may our land be bright With Free-dom's ho - ly light;

From ev' - ry—— moun - tain - side Let—— free-dom ring.
My heart—— with—— rap - ture thrills Like—— that a - bove.
Let rocks—— their—— si - lence break, The—— sound pro - long.
Pro - tect—— us—— by Thy might, Great—— God, our King!

Variations on "America" (excerpts)

by Charles Ives

Musical variations are different versions of the same tune. Ives wrote these variations as a teenager. The music is humorous and somewhat outrageous. One section of the music is in two different keys at the same time—one key in the right hand and another in the left.

LISTENING MAP *You will hear the basic theme, followed by variations. Listen for the dramatic changes and playful surprises.*

FRIGHT NIGHT

The fun of fright and "things that go bump in the night" makes Halloween a playful holiday.

THE BOOGIE WOOGIE GHOST

Words and Music by
Nadine M. Peglar

1. There was a ghost on Hal-low-een, He real-ly made the ghost-ie scene,
2. He'd go out spook-ing late at night, And giv-ing ev'-ry-one a fright,

He was the Boo-gie-Woo-gie Ghost, He was the ghost-ie with the most,
He knew some wit-ches, two or three, And they would all go on a spree,

And when the kid-dies came a-round, He'd give out with a ghost-ly sound,
And when the morn-ing came a-round, He'd give one last mys-te-rious sound,

He'd go, "Boo-oo-oo-oo-ooo."
ooo."

Though he real - ly was - n't ver - y spook - y, ——

Kids all thought that he was rath - er cool.

E - ven though he was a lit - tle kook - y, ——

He was just a spe - cial —— ghoul. When you're

out on Hal - low - een And he ap - pears up - on the scene,

Don't give a scream and run a - way, Just ask him if he'll stay and play.

You'll like the Boo - gie - Woo - gie Ghost, He'll be the one you dig the most,

You'll love his Boo - oo - oo - oo - ooo.

Whisper a spooky vocal
ostinato to help express the
chilling message of this song.

The Ghost of JOHN

Words and Music
by Martha Grubb

Have you seen the ghost of John?

Long white bones with the skin all gone, ———— Oo, oo, ——

Would-n't it be chil-ly with no skin on!

Theme in YELLOW

I spot the hills
With yellow balls in autumn.
I light the prairie cornfields
Orange and tawny gold clusters
And I am called pumpkins.
On the last of October
When dusk is fallen
Children join hands
And circle round me
Singing ghost songs
And love to the harvest moon;
I am a jack-o'-lantern
With terrible teeth
And the children know
I am fooling.

—*Carl Sandburg*

LISTENING

Scary Music Montage

A suspense film or television program uses scary music to heighten the effect of what is happening on the screen. The frightening effect of music, however, is not only used in television and film. For a long time, composers have used minor keys, crescendos, and surprises to build tension and startle their listeners. As you listen to the "Scary Music Montage," you will hear music that makes you feel uneasy. Determine why the music might have an unsettling effect.

The rhythm of this song may get your skeleton moving!

DRY BONES

African American Spiritual

A Freely

E - ze-kiel cried, "Them dry bones!" E - ze-kiel cried, "Them dry bones!"

E - ze-kiel cried, "Them dry bones, Now hear the Word of the Lord!" E -

gradually getting faster

B

Lord!" The foot bone con-nect-ed to the leg bone,

The leg bone con-nect-ed to the knee bone,

The knee bone con-nect-ed to the hip-bone,

The hip-bone con-nect-ed to the back-bone,

GIVE THANKS

Every day of the year, crops are gathered somewhere in the world. Whenever and wherever the harvest comes, it is a time for celebration and thanksgiving.

For Health and Strength

Old English Round

For health and strength and dai - ly food

We praise Thy name, Oh, Lord.

During the 1800s, there were many Shaker villages in the eastern part of the United States. Kathy Jakobsen's painting, shown below, depicts the simple life-style of Shaker communities. This Shaker song welcomes visitors.

A Mince Pie or Pudding

Shaker Song

Wel - come here! Wel - come here!

All be a - live and be of good cheer!

I've got a pie all baked com - plete with

*Go back to the beginning and sing to the end
(Da Capo al Fine)*

pud - ding, too, that's ver - y sweet.

North Union, Shaker Village, Kathy Jakobsen, 1984

Winter Carnival

Winters are very cold in Canada. Each year, however, Canadians of all ages gather to "discover the warmth of winter" at the Quebec Carnival. Parades, fireworks, snow sculpture competitions, sporting events, and concerts are all part of the winter celebration. The festivities are led by Bonhomme Carnaval, a smiling snowman.

Bonhomme! Bonhomme!

Canadian Folk Song
English Version by MMH

Bonhomme Carnaval is the official ambassador of the Quebec Carnival.

C7 F

là? Sais - tu jou - er de ce vi - o - lon - là?
la sɛ tü ʒu e də sə vi ɔ lɔ̃ la
lin? Can you play this on the vi - o - lin?
flute? Can you play this on the ti - ny flute?
drum? Can you play this on the big—— bass drum?

verses accumulate

F Bb F

Zing, zing, zing de ce vi - o - lon - là. Bon - homme! Bon -
ʒɛ̃ ʒɛ̃ ʒɛ̃ də sə vi ɔ lɔ̃ la bɔ nɔm bɔ
Zing, zing, zing on the vi - o - lin. Bon - homme! Bon -
Toot, toot, toot on the ti - ny flute,
Boom, boom, boom on the big—— bass drum,

Bb

homme! Tu n'es pas maîtr' dans ta mai -
nɔm tü ne pɑ mɛtr dɑ̃ ta mɛ
homme! You are not boss in your own

Bb Eb F7 Bb

son Quand nous y som - mes!————
ʒɔ̃ kɑ̃ nu zi sɔ mə
home When we come here to play!————

4. Can you play this on the great big horn?
   Ta-ta-ra on the great big horn, . . .

Add a partner song to "Jingle Bells" to create harmony.

WINTER FANTASY

Words and Music
by Jill Gallina

do — Snow - flakes fall - ing all o - ver town,

do — Dash - ing through the snow in a one - horse o - pen sleigh,

Slip - ping, slid - ing ev' - ry - bod - y rush - in' 'round.

O'er the fields we go, laugh - ing all the way.

There's an i - cy chill in the air,

Bells on bob - tails ring, mak - ing spir - its bright. What

Tell - ing us that win - ter's real - ly here. Oh!

fun it is to laugh and sing a sleigh - ing song to - night. Oh!

The Miracle of Lights

Lighting candles for Hanukkah honors a special event in Jewish history. Long ago, the people of Jerusalem wanted to relight their holy lamp, but there was only enough oil for one day. Miraculously, the small amount of oil lasted for eight days.

IN THE WINDOW

Hebrew Folk Song
Arranged by Mary Goetze

Slowly

In the win-dow where you can see the glow of my me-no-rah on new-ly fall-en snow, I will set you one* lit-tle can-dle(s) on this, the {first* / last} night of Ha-nuk-kah.

*On each of the nights of Hanukkah, sing the correct number.
On the eighth verse, sing the word "last."

280

Add this part to some of the verses.

In the win - dow, see the glow,_____ my me - no - rah can - dles this night of Ha - nuk- kah.

Add this part to some other verses. Try singing all three parts together.

In the win - dow where you can see the glow, my me - no- rah on the fal - len snow. I will set____ my lit - tle can-dles on this____ night of Ha - nuk- kah.

MEXICAN CHRISTMAS SEASON

In Mexico and the southwestern United States, *Las Posadas* is a highlight of the Christmas season. The celebration begins on December 16 and lasts nine nights until Christmas Eve. Songs tell the story of Mary and Joseph's trip to Bethlehem.

There are two parts to "Para pedir posada." The first part of the song is a question, the second an answer. As the song begins, Joseph asks for shelter. The answer is that there is no room.

Para pedir posada

Mexican Folk Song
English Version by MMH

Spanish:	En	nom-bre	del	cie	- lo,	Os	pi -
Pronunciation:	en	nom bɾe	ðel	sye	lo	os	pi
English:	In	the name	of Heav	- en,		Hear	my

do	po - sa	- da,	Pues	no	pue - de	an -
ðo	po sa	ða	pwes	no	pwe ðe	an
plea	for shel	- ter,	My	poor wife is	wea	-

Each evening of *Las Posadas*, groups of friends walk from home to home, stopping to sing. Mary and Joseph are tired and need a place to rest. The word posada actually means "inn or shelter." The people at home answer, but the travelers are not allowed to come in.

At last, after being turned away again and again,
Mary and Joseph are welcomed.

Entren santos peregrinos

Enter, Holy Pilgrims

Mexican Folk Song
English Version by MMH

Spanish: En - tren san - tos pe - re - gri - nos, pe - re - gri - nos,— Re - ci -
Pronunciation: en tren san tos pe ɾe gɾi nos pe ɾe gɾi nos ɾe si
English: En - ter in, all ho - ly pil - grims, ho - ly pil - grims.— Wel - come

ban es - te rin - cón, que aun - que es po - bre la mo - ra - da, la mo -
βan es te rin koen keaun kes po βɾe la mo ɾa ða la mo
to our hum - ble grove. There is lit - tle we can give you, we can

ra - da,— Os la doy de co - ra - zón.
ɾa ða os la ðoi ðe ko ɾa son
give you,— Still we wel - come you with love.

When the posadas procession ends, the owner of the home opens the door, and everyone comes in for a festive party that includes breaking a piñata.

Dale, dale, dale!

Mexican Folk Song
English Version by MMH

Verse

Spanish: En las no - ches de po - sa - das,
Pronunciation: en las no ches ðe po sa ðas
English: On the nights of *Las Po - sa - das,*

la pi - ña - ta es lo me - jor,
la pi nya taes lo me xor
chil - dren laugh and try with all their might,

Y los ni - ños más a - le - gres
i los ni nyos mas a le gres
To win the bright *pi - ña - ta's* trea -

le pe - gan con gran fer - vor.
le pe gang kong gran fer βor
sure they swing and swing all night.

Refrain

C   F   G7   C

Da - le, da - le, da - le,   no pier - das el   ti - no,
ða le ða le ða   le   no pyeɾ ðas el ti   no
Da - le, da - le, da - le,   do not lose *el*   *ti - no,*

C   F   G7   C

Mi - de la dis - tan - cia, que hay en el ca - mi - no.
mi ðe la ðis tan sya keai en el ka mi no
Turn a - round and find it on___ *el ca - mi - no.*

C   F   G7   C

Que si no le das   de un pa - lo - te pi - no,
ke si no le ðas   ðeun pa lo te pi no
For if you should miss it   with *pa - lo - te*   *pi - no,*

C   F   G7   C

Por - que tie - nes ca - ra, de pu - ro pe - pi - no.___
poɾ ke tye nes ka ɾa ðe pu ɾo pe pi no
You will feel as fool - ish as *pu - ro pe -* *pi - no.*___

NOEL, NOEL

This song is from the program *Rudolph, the Red-Nosed Reindeer.*

A Holly Jolly Christmas

Words and Music
by Johnny Marks

Have a hol - ly jol - ly Christ - mas, it's the best time of the year.

I don't know if there'll be snow but have a cup of cheer.

Have a hol - ly jol - ly Christ - mas, and when you walk down the street

Say hel - lo to friends you know and ev' - ry - one you meet.

Oh, ho, the mis - tle - toe hung where you can see.

Some - bod - y waits for you, kiss her once for me.

Have a hol-ly jol-ly Christ-mas, and in case you did-n't hear,

Oh, by gol-ly, have a hol-ly jol-ly Christ-mas this year. Have a

Christ-mas _____ this year. _____

In Italy, during the nine days before Christmas, people celebrate with fairs, fireworks, and bonfires. The Christmas Eve celebration honors the birth of Jesus with prayers and carols. This Italian carol is a lullaby for the baby.

Dormi, dormi

Sleep, Sleep

Italian Carol
English Text
by George K. Evans

Verse *mp*

Italian: Dor - mi, dor - mi, bel bam - bin. Re di - vin, re di - vin.
Pronunciation: dor mi dor mi bel bam bin re di vin re di vin
English: Sleep, O sleep, my love - ly child. King di - vine, king di - vine.

Fà la nan - na, fan - to - li - no. Re di - vin, re di - vin.
fa la nan na fan to li no re di vin re di vin
Close your eyes and sweet - ly slum - ber. King di - vine, king di - vine.

Fà la nan - na, fan - to - li - no. Fa - la - la - la -
fa la nan na fan to li no
Close your eyes and sweet - ly slum - ber.

la - la - la - la - la, Fa - la - la - la - la - la - la - la, Fa - la - la - la - la - la,

Fa - la - la - la - la - la, Fa - la - la - la - la - la, Fa - la - la - la. Fa - la - la - la.

According to the Christmas story, three wise men, or kings, brought gifts to the newborn child on January 6. In Latin American countries, this day is known as Three Kings Day. It is the day that children receive gifts.

We Three Kings

Words and Music
by John Henry Hopkins

Verse

Em   B   Em

We three kings of O - ri - ent are,
Bear - ing gifts we trav - erse a - far,

Em   D   G

Field and foun - tain, moor and moun - tain,

B7   Em

Fol - low - ing yon - der star.

Refrain

D   G   C   G

O _____ Star of won - der, star of night,
Star with roy - al beau - ty bright,

G   D   C   D   G

West - ward lead - ing, still pro - ceed - ing,

G   C   G

Guide us to thy per - fect light.

There are twelve days between Christmas and Epiphany, the day when the three kings arrived with their gifts.

The Twelve Days of Christmas

English Carol

1. On the first day of Christ-mas my true love sent to me: A par-tridge— in a pear tree. 2. On the sec-ond day of Christ-mas my true love sent to me: Two tur-tle doves, and a par-tridge— in a pear tree. 3. On the third day of Christ-mas my true love sent to me: Three French—hens, two tur-tle doves, and a par-tridge— in a pear tree. 4. On the fourth day of Christ-mas my true love sent to me:

Four col-ly birds, two tur-tle doves, and a par-tridge in a pear
three French hens,

tree. 5. On the fifth day of Christ-mas my true love sent to me:

Five gold-en rings, four col-ly birds, three French hens,

two tur-tle doves, and a par-tridge in a pear tree.

End (Fine)

6.-12. On the sixth day of Christ-mas my true love sent to me:
(seventh, etc.)

Go back to the sign and sing to the end
(Del Segno al Fine)

6. Six geese a-lay-ing,

7. Seven swans a-swimming,

8. Eight maids a-milking,

9. Nine drummers drumming,

10. Ten pipers piping,

11. Eleven ladies dancing,

12. Twelve lords a-leaping,

ASIAN NEW

For Asians and Asian Americans, celebrating the new year may last for several weeks. The exact date of the holiday depends upon each country's traditions.

In Vietnam and China, the Kitchen God goes to the heavens and reports on the family at the end of the old year. After cleaning and decorating the house, families send the Kitchen God off with firecrackers, food, and gifts in hopes of a good report.

In Vietnam, the new year celebration is called Tet. During the first days of the new year everyone tries to be happy. To be angry could bring bad luck.

Buying mume blossoms is part of preparing for Tet.

YEAR CELEBRATIONS

In Laos, the new year usually begins in April. In preparation, houses and temples are washed. Splashing and throwing water becomes a festive part of the celebration. People are joyful because they believe that the happier you are, the happier the year to come will be.

Suk san wan pi mai
New Year's Song

Laotian Song
Collected and Transcribed by
Kathy B. Sorensen
English Version by MMH

Preparation for the Chinese New Year begins at least a month in advance. In addition to cleaning the house, families paint their front doors red—the color red means happiness. When the new year actually arrives, the celebration lasts for fifteen days.

LISTENING

Chinese Lion Dance *Chinese Folk Music*

On the third to fifth days of the Chinese New Year, the Chinese Lion dances through the crowds in the streets. Martial-arts students perform the lion dance. Listen to the rhythm of the Chinese drum and cymbal.

Lion Dance Drum Pattern

Lion Dance Cymbal Pattern

The lion asleep.

The lion awakening.

The Chinese Lion, danced by students of the Wan Chi Ming Hung Gar Institute in New York City.

The lion bowing.

Dr. King's DREAM

The powerful speeches of Dr. Martin Luther King, Jr., inspired many people to work for equal rights. His words still give people hope and encouragement.

Martin's Cry

Words and Music by Vernon Clark

1. There was a man— named Mar - tin Lu - ther King, who said,
2. King took a stand— for civ - il rights a - cross the land,
3. King led a march— to Wash - ing - ton and said a - gain,

"Let free - dom ring!
Let free - dom ring!
"Let free - dom ring!"

I have a dream— that one day this na - tion will
No mat - ter where— his foot - steps led him, he would
He gave his life— so one day all peo - ple could

In 1983, the birthday of Martin Luther King, Jr., became a national holiday. It is a day to celebrate his dream of equality for all people. People sing songs like this African American spiritual to honor Dr. King's belief in peace and freedom.

DOWN BY THE RIVERSIDE

African American Spiritual

Verse

1. Gon-na lay down my sword and shield,
2. Gon-na lay down my bur - den,
3. Gon-na try on my star - ry crown, } Down by the riv-er-side,
4. Gon-na meet my dear old fath - er,
5. Gon-na meet my dear old moth - er,

Down by the riv-er - side, Down by the riv-er - side,

Gon-na lay down my sword and shield,
Gon-na lay down my bur - den,
Gon-na try on my star - ry crown, } Down by the riv-er-side,
Gon-na meet my dear old fath - er,
Gon-na meet my dear old moth - er,

Gon-na stud-y war no more.

Refrain

I ain't gon-na stud-y war no more,

Ain't gon-na stud-y war no more,

Ain't gon-na stud-y war no more,

stud-y war no more.

...UNTIL JUSTICE ROLLS DOWN LIKE WATERS
AND RIGHTEOUSNESS LIKE A MIGHTY STREAM

MARTIN LUTHER KING Jr.

The Civil Rights Memorial in Montgomery, Alabama, was designed by Maya Lin.
Ms. Lin also designed the Vietnam Memorial in Washington, D.C.

A Great President

Abraham Lincoln was the sixteenth
president of the United States. During
the Civil War, his leadership freed the
slaves and reunited the country. The
wisdom and understanding of Abraham
Lincoln were expressed in his speeches.

Lincoln Portrait

(excerpts) *by Aaron Copland*

Lincoln Portrait was the result of Aaron Copland's being asked to write a musical portrait of a great American. When he started, he was concerned that it would be difficult for his music to express the greatness of Abraham Lincoln. He solved the problem by using Lincoln's letters and speeches as the text. Copland's music frames Abraham Lincoln's own words. You will hear a full orchestra and a soloist who speaks those words.

To Meet MR. LINCOLN

If I lived at the time
That Mr. Lincoln did,
And I met Mr. Lincoln
With his stovepipe lid

And his coalblack cape
And his thundercloud beard,
And worn and sad-eyed
He appeared:

"Don't worry, Mr. Lincoln,"
I'd reach up and pat his hand,
"We've got a fine President
For this land;

And the Union will be saved,
And the slaves will go free;
And you will live forever
In our nation's memory."

— *Eve Merriam*

Celebrations *Presidents' Day* **303**

MARCHING ON

Macnamara's Band

Music by Shamus O'Connor
Words by John J. Stamford

Verse

1. Oh! me name is Mac - na - mar - a, I'm the lead - er of the band,——
2. Right—— now we are re - hears - in', for a ver - y swell af - fair,——
3. Oh! my name is Un - cle Yul - ius and from Swe - den I have come,——
4. Oh! I wear a bunch of sham - rocks and a un - i - form of green,——

Al - though we're few in num - bers we're the fin - est in the land.
The an - nual cel - e - bra - tion, all the gen - try will be there.
To play with Mac - na - mar - a's band and beat the big bass drum,
And I'm the fun - niest look - ing Swede that you have ev - er seen.

We play at wakes and wed - dings and at
When Gen - 'ral Grant to Ire - land came he
And when I march a - long the street the
There's O' - Bri - ens and Ry - ans and Shee - hans and Mee - hans, they

ev' - ry fan - cy ball,—— And when we play to
took me by the hand,—— Says he, "I nev - er
la - dies think I'm grand,—— They shout, "There's Un - cle
come from Ire - land,—— But by Yim - min - y I'm the

304

ST. PATRICK'S DAY

fu - ner - als we play the march from Saul.
saw the likes of Mac - na - mar - a's band."
Yul - ius play - ing with an I - rish band."
on - ly Swede in Mac - na - mar - a's band.

Refrain

Oh! the drums go bang, and the cym - bals clang, and the horns they blaze a -

way;— Mc - Car - thy pumps the old ba - zoon whIle I the pipes do play;

And, Hen - nes - sey Ten - nes - see too - tles the flute, and the mu - sic is some - thin'

grand;— A cred - it to old Ire - land is Mac - na - mar - a's band.

Arbor Day
PLANT A TREE

Trees improve our soil, air, and water and give us food and paper. Just as important, they provide shade and beauty. We plant trees to enjoy their benefits for years to come.

THE OAK OF VERCINGETORIX

Gustave Courbet (1819–1877), a French painter, named this painting for a strong Roman leader. The subject is an oak tree. Oak trees live as long as 400 years and produce wood that is heavy, hard, and strong.

"The Ash Grove" comes from Wales. The song describes the beauty of a group or grove of trees.

THE ASH GROVE

Welsh Folk Song

1. Down yon-der green val-ley where stream-lets me-an-der,
   Or at the bright noon-tide in sol-i-tude wan-der
2. The ash-grove, how grace-ful, how plain-ly 'tis speak-ing,
   When-ev-er the light through its branch-es is break-ing,

When twi-light is fad-ing I pen-sive-ly rove,
A-mid the dark shades of the lone-ly ash grove.
The harp through it play-ing has lan-guage for me;
A host of kind fac-es is gaz-ing on me;

'Tis there where the black-bird is cheer-ful-ly sing-ing,
The friends of my child-hood a-gain are be-fore me,

Each war-bler en-chants with his note from the tree.
Each step wakes a mem-'ry as free-ly I roam;

Ah, then lit-tle think I of sor-row or sad-ness;
With soft whis-pers la-den, its leaves rus-tle o'er me,

The ash grove en-chant-ing spells beau-ty for me.
The ash grove, the ash grove a-lone is my home.

All over the world, people have holidays to honor trees. Tu bi Sh'vat is a Jewish holiday–the "New Year for Trees." In Israel, children plant trees on this holiday. Trees are important in a dry, hot country because they provide shade and keep the soil from washing away. They also offer food, beauty, and oxygen to breathe.

Hashkëdiya
The Almond Tree

Jewish Folk Song
English Version by MMH

Counting Out
RHYME

Silver bark of beech, and sallow
Bark of yellow birch, and yellow
Twig of willow.

Stripe of green in moosewood maple,
Color seen in leaf of apple,
Bark of popple.

Wood of popple pale as moonbeam,
Wood of oak for yoke and barn-beam,
Wood of hornbeam.

Silver bark of beech, and hollow
Stem of elder, tall and yellow
Twig of willow.

—Edna St. Vincent Millay

LISTENING

Feuilles Mortes *by Claude Debussy*

Debussy's music has a beautiful sound. The harmonies shift gently and blend together. This style is known as musical impressionism. The title of this piano piece means "Dead Leaves." As you listen, you will hear floating sounds that bring to mind softly falling leaves.

BABYLON'S FALLIN'

Virginia Folk Song

Bab - y - lon's fall - in', fall - in', fall - in',

Bab - y - lon's fall - in' to rise no more.

PAGE'S TRAIN

North Carolina Folk Song

Pa - ge's train runs so fast,

Can't see noth - ing but the win - dow glass.

Kentucky Folk Song

Refrain

Down the road and a-cross the creek,

Can't get a let-ter but once a week.

Verse

I - da Red, I - da Blue,
I - da Red, I - da Green,
I - da Red, I - da Gold,
I - da Red, I - da Red,

I got stuck on I - da too.
pret-ti - est girl you've ev - er seen.
she is some - thin' to be - hold.
that girl's sweet-er than gin - ger - bread.

Lady, Come Down and See

Traditional Round

La - dy, come down and see, the cat sits in the plum tree.

GOOD-BYE MY RILEY O

African American Song
from the Georgia Sea Islands
Collected and Adapted by Lydia A. Parrish

1. Ri - ley, Ri - ley, where are you?
2. Ri - ley gone to Liv - er - pool.
3. Ri - ley gone to Lon - don Town.
4. Ri - ley gone to Mo - bile Bay.

O Ri - ley O man!

Ri - ley gone and I goin' too, Good - bye my Ri - ley O!

Before Dinner

Zairian Folk Song

Call
Response

First we go to hoe our gar - den, }
Next we car - ry jugs of wa - ter, } Ya, ya, ya, ya.

Call
Response

Then we pound the yel - low corn, }
Then we stir our pots of mush, } Ya, ya, ya, ya.

Call
Response

Now we eat, come gath - er 'round the camp - fire, Ya, ya, ya, ya.

Oliver Cromwell

English Folk Song

1. Ol - i - ver Crom-well lay bur-ied and dead, Hee haw,
(2.) ap-ples were ripe___ and read-y to fall, Hee haw,
(3.) sad-dle and bri-dle, they lie on the shelf, Hee haw,

bur - ied and dead. There grew an old ap - ple tree
read - y to fall. There came an old wo - man to
lie on the shelf. If you want an - y more you can

o - ver his head, Hee haw, o - ver his head. 2. The
gath - er them all, Hee haw, gath - er them all. 3. The
sing it your-self, Hee haw, sing it your-self.

Shaker Song

Hop up and jump up and whirl 'round, whirl 'round,

Gath - er love, here it is all 'round, all 'round,

314

Here is love flow-ing 'round, catch it as you whirl round,

Reach up and reach down, here it is all 'round.

San lun tsa

Three-Wheeled Taxi

Taiwanese Folk Song
Collected and Transcribed by Kathy B. Sorensen
English Version by MMH

Mandarin: 三 輪 車 跑 得 快 上 面 坐 個 老 太 太
Pronunciation: san luɛn chər pau di kwai san miɛn juɔ gər lau tai tai
English: **Shall I come?— Shall I go? East or West I do not know!**

要 五 毛 給 一 塊 你 說 奇 怪 不 奇 怪
yau wu mao gei yi kwai ni shuɔ chi gwai bu chi gwai
I am lost— all a-lone,— Three-wheeled tax-i,— take me home!

LONDON'S BURNING

Traditional English Round

Lon-don's burn - ing, Lon-don's burn - ing, Fetch the en - gines, fetch the en - gines, Fire! Fire! Fire! Fire! Pour on wa - ter, pour on wa - ter.

Push the Business On

English Singing Game

We'll hire a horse and grab a rig; And all the world will dance a jig;

And we will do what - ev - er we can to push the busi-ness on.——

316

Korobushka

Russian Folk Song
Russian Words by Nikolay Kekrasov
English Version by MMH

Waltzing Matilda

Music Adapted by Marie Cowan
Words Adapted from A. "Banjo" Paterson

Verse

1. Once a jol-ly swag-man camp'd— by a bil-la-bong,
2. Down— came a jum-buck to drink— at that bil-la-bong,
3. Up— came the stock-man, mount-ed on his thor-ough-bred,
4. Up— jumped the swag-man, sprang in-to the bil-la-bong,

Un-der the shade of a coo-li-bah tree, And he
Up jumped the swag-man and grabbed him with glee, And he
Down came the troop-ers,— one,— two, three.
"You'll nev-er catch me a-live,"— said he, And his

sang as he watched and wait-ed till his bil-ly boiled,
sang as he shoved that jum-buck in his tuck-er-bag,
"Who's that jol-ly jum-buck you've got in your tuck-er-bag?
ghost may be heard as you pass— by that bil-la-bong,

"You'll come a waltz-ing, Ma-til-da with me."

Refrain

Waltz-ing Ma-til-da, waltz-ing Ma-til-da, "You'll come a waltz-ing Ma-til - da with me."

And he sang   as   he watched and
And he sang   as   he shoved that
"Who's that jol - ly jum - buck
And his ghost   may be heard as you

wait - ed till his bil - ly boiled,
jum - buck in his tuck- er bag,
you've got in your tuck- er bag?"
pass—— by that bil - la- bong,

"You'll come a waltz-ing, Ma - til- da, with me."

Swagman–a hobo

Billabong–a water hole in a dried-up riverbed

Billy–tin can used as a kettle to boil water

Waltzing Matilda–the bundle on a stick carried by a
    swagman

Jumbuck–a small lamb

Tuckerbag–a knapsack

Stockman–a person who owns or works with livestock

Ah, Poor Bird

Old English Melody

1. Ah, poor bird, take your flight, Far a-bove the sor-rows of this   sad night.
2. Ah, poor bird,   as   you   fly, Can you see the dawn of to-mor- row's sky?

From GROWING WITH MUSIC, Book 3 TE, by Wilson et al. © 1970
Prentice-Hall, Inc., Englewood Cliffs, NJ. Arrangement adapted.

The California Song

American Folk Song

Verse

D

1. We've formed our band and we are all well manned
2. Oh, the gold in thar— most— an - y - whar,
3. Oh don't you cry— or— heave a sigh,
4. We ex - pect our share— of the coars - est fare,

D   A7   D

To jour - ney a - far to the pro - mised land,
They dig it— out with an i - ron bar,
For we'll come— back a - gain— bye and bye,
And some - times— sleep in the o - pen air,

D

Where the gold - en ore is thick in store
And— where it's thick with a spade and pick,
Don't have fear or shed a tear,
Up on the cold ground we will sleep— sound,

D   A7   D

On the banks of the Sac - ra - men - to shore,
They've— ta-ken out— lumps as big as a brick.
But— pa-tient - ly— wait for a - bout two year.
Ex - cept when the wolves come howl - ing round.

Refrain D   G   D

Then ho, boys, ho! to Cal - i - for - nia go,

320

for the moun-tains bold are cov-ered with gold on the

banks of the Sac-ra - men - to,

Heigh, ho a - way we go,

Dig - ging up gold in Fris - co.

Troika Song

Music by Sergei Prokofiev
Words by Phyllis Stycos

We're rid-ing in a three-horse sleigh to - day. The

snow is so spark-ling and bright! In our three-horse sleigh we'll

ride all through the day. And we'll ride half-way through the night.

I Love the Mountains

Traditional Round

I love the moun-tains, I love the roll-ing hills,

I love the flow-ers, I love the daf-fo-dils;

I love the fire-side when all the lights are low.

Boom-dee-ah-da, Boom-dee-ah-da, Boom-dee-ah-da, Boom-dee-ah-da.

When I First Came to This Land

Words and Music by Oscar Brand

Verse

1.–5. When I first came to this land, I was not a wealth-y man.

Then I built my-self a shack.
Then I bought my-self a cow.
Then I bought my-self a horse.
Then I got my-self a wife.
Then I got my-self a son.

I did what I could.____

Repeat these four measures for additional lines in verses 2-5

I
called my shack *Break - my - back.*
called my cow *No - milk - now,*
called my horse *Lame - of - course,*
called my wife *Joy - of - my - life.*
told my son *My work's done.*
I

Refrain

Still the land was sweet and good, I did what I could.____

Golden Ring Around the Susan Girl

Southern Appalachian Folk Song
New Words and Music by Jean Ritchie

Verse

1. Gold - en ring a - round the Su - san girl,
2. Do - si - do right, you Su - san girl,
3. Hand o -ver hand, you Su - san girl,
(4.) take 'im on home, Su - san girl,

Gold - en ring a-round the Su - san girl, Gold - en ring a-round the
Do - si - do right, you Su - san girl, Do - si - do right, you
Hand o -ver hand, you Su - san girl, Hand o -ver hand, you
Take 'im on home, Su - san girl, Take 'im on home,

Su - san girl, All the way a -round the Su - san girl.
Su - san girl, All the way a -round the Su - san girl. And
Su - san girl, All the way a -round the Su - san girl.
Su - san girl, All the way a -round the Su - san girl. Then

Take a lit - tle girl and give 'er a whirl,
do - si - do left, you Su - san girl,
Get a lit - tle fas - ter, Su - san girl,
take 'im on home, Su - san girl,

Take a lit - tle girl and give 'er a whirl, Take a lit - tle girl and
Do - si - do left, you Su - san girl, Do - si - do left, you
Get a lit - tle fas - ter, Su - san girl, Get a lit - tle fas - ter,
Take 'im on home, Su - san girl, Take 'im on home,

give'er a whirl,
Su - san girl,
Su - san girl,
Su - san girl,

All the way a-round the Su-san girl.

Refrain

'Round and a-round, Su - san girl, 'Round and a-round, Su - san girl,

'Round and a-round, Su-san girl, All the way a-round the Su-san girl.

4. Then

English Melody

do

Hey, ho! No-bod-y home. Meat nor drink nor

mon-ey have I none. Yet will I be ver - y ver-y mer-ry.

Coda

Hey, ho! No - bod - y home.

When I Was a Lad

Music by Arthur S. Sullivan
Words by William S. Gilbert

Leader B♭   F

1. When I was a lad I served a term As
2. As of-fice boy I made such a mark That they
3. Now, lands-men all, who-ev-er you may be, If you

E♭dim   F7

of - fice boy to an at - tor - ney's firm; I
gave me the post of a jun - ior clerk; I
want to rise to the top of the tree, If your

B♭   F

cleaned the win-dows and I swept the floor, And I
served the writs with a smile so bland, And I
soul is -n't fet - tered to an of - fice stool, Be

C7   F7   *Group*

pol-ished up the han - dle of the big front door. He
cop - ied all the let - ters in a big round hand; He
care - ful to be guid - ed by this gold - en rule: Be

F7   C7   F7   *Leader*

pol-ished up the han - dle of the big front door. I
cop - ied all the let - ters in a big round hand; I
care - ful to be guid - ed by this gold - en rule: Stick

pol- ished up the han - dle so care - ful - lee That
cop - ied all the let - ters in a hand so free That
close——— to your desks,——— and nev- er go to sea, And you

now I am the rul - er of the Queen's Na - vee. He
now I am the rul - er of the Queen's Na - vee. He
all——— may be rul - ers of the Queen's Na - vee. Stick

Group

pol- ished up the han - dle so care - ful - lee That
cop - ied all the let - ters in a hand so free That
close——— to your desks——— and nev- er go to sea, And you

now he is the rul - er of the Queen's Na - vee.
now he is the rul - er ot the Queen's Na - vee.
all——— may be rul - ers of the Queen's Na - vee.

Orchestra Song

Austrian Round

1. The vi - o - lin's ring - ing like

2. The clar - i - net, the clar - i - net plays

3. The trum - pet is sound - ing ta ta ta

love - ly — sing - ing, The vi - o - lin's

doo - dle, doo - dle, doo - dle, doo - dle det, The clar - i - net, the

ta ta ta ta ta ta ta ta ta ta, The trum - pet is

ring - ing   like   love - - - - ly —— song.

clar - i - net   plays   doo- dle,   doo- dle, doo- dle det.

sound - ing ta ta ta   ta   ta ta ta   ta   ta   ta   ta.

Add these parts to the first three.

4 The horn,   the horn   a - wakes me   at   morn.

5 The drum's play - ing two tones and   al - ways the same tones,

Five,   one,   one,   five,   five,   five, five, five,   one.

Oh, Won't You Sit Down?

Freely
Refrain

African American Spiritual

Oh, won't you sit down?— Lord, I can't sit down.—

Oh, won't you sit down?— Lord, I can't sit down.—

Oh, won't you sit down?— Lord, I can't sit down.—

End
(Fine)

'Cause I just got to Heav-en, gon-na look a-round.—

Verse *Call*   *Response*

1. Who's that yon-der dressed in red?— Must be the child-ren that—
2. Who's that yon-der dressed in blue?— Must be the child-ren that are

Call

Mo-ses led.— Who's that yon-der dressed in white?—
com-in' through.— Who's that yon-der dressed in black?—

Last time, go back to the beginning
and sing to the end
(Da Capo al Fine)

Response

Must be the child-ren of the Is-rael-ite.—
Must be the hy-po-crites a-turn-in' back.—

330

THE DERBY RAM

English Folk Song
Ozark Version

Verse

1. As I went down to Der - by town, all
2. The wool up - on this ram's____ back It
3. The horns up - on this ram's____ head They
4. The ears up - on this ram's____ head They
5. Oh ev' - ry tooth this ram____ had would

on a sum - mer's day,____ It's there I saw the
drug____ to the ground,____ I hauled it to the
reached____ to the moon,____ the butch - er went up on
reached____ to the sky,____ the ea - gle built his
hold a bush - el of corn,____ And ev' - ry foot he

fin - est ram, that's ev - er fed on hay.____
mar - ket, And it weighed ten thou - sand pounds.____
Feb - ru - ar - y, And nev - er got back till June.____
nest there, For I heard the young ones cry.____
stood____ on, Would cov - er an a - cre of ground.____

Refrain

And if you don't be - lieve me,____ And think I tell a lie,____

Just you go down to Der - by, And you'll see the same as I.____

I'd Like to Teach the World to Sing

Words and Music by Bill Backer,
Billy Davis, Roger Cook, and
Roger Greenaway

1. I'd like to build the world a home
(2.) like to teach the world to sing
3. I'd like to see the world for once

and fur - nish it with love,
in per - fect har - mo - ny,
all stand - ing hand in hand,

grow ap - ple trees and hon - ey bees and
I'd like to hold it in my arms and
and hear them ech - o through the hills for

snow white tur - tle doves. 2. I'd

keep it com - pa - ny. peace through - out the land.

That's the song I hear; Let the world sing to - day,

D.C. (Verse 3)

A song of peace that ech - oes on and nev - er goes a - way.

American Folk Song

OLD DAN TUCKER

Verse

G

1. Old Dan Tuck-er's a fine old man.
2. Old Dan Tuck-er be-gan in ear-ly life, To

G   D7   G

Washed his face in a fry-ing pan, Combed his head with a
play the ban-jo and the fife. He'd play the boys and

G   D7

wag-on wheel And died with a tooth-ache in his heel.
gals to sleep, And then in-to his bunk he'd creep.

Refrain

G   C   D7

Get out the way, Old Dan Tuck-er, You're too late to

G   C

get your sup-per. Sup-per's o-ver and din-ner's cook-in' And

D7   G

Old Dan Tuck-er's just stand-in' look-in'.

Grandma's Feather Bed

Words and Music by Jim Connor

Verse

1. Now when I was a lit-tle bit-ty boy Just up off— of the floor,

We used to go out to Grand-ma's house ev'-ry month end or so.—

————— We'd have chick-en pie—— and coun-try ham, and

home-made but-ter on the bread. But the best thing a-bout

Grand-ma's house was a great big feath-er bed.

Refrain

It was nine feet high and six feet wide and soft as a down-y

chick. It was made from the feath-ers of for-ty 'lev-en geese, took a whole bolt of cloth for the tick. It-'d hold eight kids and four— — hound dogs and the pig-gy we took from the shed. We did-n't get much sleep, but we had a lot of fun on Grand-ma's feath-er bed.

2. And after supper we'd sit around the fire
   and the old folks bit the shoe.
   And my Pa would talk about the farm and the war
   and my Granny'd sing a ballad or two.
   And I'd sit and listen and watch the fire till
   the cobwebs filled my head.
   The next thing I know I'll wake up in the mornin'
   In the middle of the old feather bed.
   Refrain

3. Well I love my Ma, I love my Pa
   I love Granny and Grandpa too.
   I been fishin' with my Uncle
   and I wrassle with my Cousin
   I even kissed Aunt Lou (Phew!)
   But if I ever had to make a choice
   I guess it ought to be said.
   That I'd trade them all plus the gal down the road
   For Grandma's feather bed.
   Refrain

Boll Weevil

Southern Folk Song
Arranged by Mary Goetze

Verse

1. The Boll Wee - vil am a lit - tle black bug from
2. The first time I saw Boll Wee - vil,___ He was
3. The Boll Wee - vil to the farm - er said, "You'd
4. The mer - chant took___ half the cot - ton.___ The

Mex - i - co they say. Come all the way to Tex - as just to
sit - tin' on the square. The next time I saw Boll Wee - vil, He had
bet - ter leave me a - lone. I done eat all your cot - ton, Now I'm
Boll Wee - vil took the rest. He on - ly left the farm - er Just a

Refrain

find a place to stay.
his whole fam' - ly there.
start - in' on your corn."
sin - gle rag - ged vest.

Just a look - in' for a home.

Just a look - in' for a home.

Just a look - in' for a home.

Just a look - in' for a home.

Donna, Donna

Music by Sholom Secunda
Words by Aaron Zeitlin

Verse

1. On a wag - on bound for mar - ket,
2. "Stop com - plain - ing," said the farm - er,
3. Calves are eas - i - ly bound and slaugh - tered,

there's a calf with a mourn - ful eye, High a - bove__ him
"who told you a__ calf to be, Why don't you__ have
nev - er know - ing the rea - son why, But who - ev - er

there's a swal - low wing - ing swift - ly__ through the sky.
wings to fly__ with, like the swal - low so proud and free?"
treas - ures free - dom, like the swal - low has learned to fly.

Refrain

How the winds are laugh - ing, they laugh with all their might,

Laugh and laugh the whole day through, and half the sum - mer's night.

Don - na, don - na, don-na, don - na, Don - na, don-na, don-na,__ don.

Don - na, don - na, don-na, don - na, Don - na, don - na, don - na, don.

Texas, Our Texas

Music by William J. Marsh
Words by Gladys Yoakum Wright

Verse *mf*

1. Tex-as, our Tex-as! All hail the might-y state!
2. Tex-as, O Tex-as! Your free-born sin-gle star,
3. Tex-as, dear Tex-as! From ty-rant grip now free!

Tex-as, our Tex-as! So won-der-ful, so great!
Sends out its ra-diance To na-tions near and far,
Shines forth in splen-dor Your star of des-ti-ny!

Bold-est and grand-est, With-stand-ing ev'-ry test; O
Em-blem of free-dom! It sets our hearts a-glow, With
Moth-er of he-roes! We come your chil-dren true, Pro -

Em-pire wide and glo-rious, You stand su-preme-ly blest.
thoughts of San Ja-cin-to And glo-rious Al-a-mo.
claim-ing our al-le-giance, Our faith our love for you.

Refrain

God bless you Tex-as! And keep you brave and strong, That

you may grow in pow'r and worth, Through-out the a-ges long.

God bless you Tex-as! And keep you brave and strong, That you may grow in pow'r and worth, Through-out the ag - es long.

1.,2.,3. *Third time, repeat Refrain and go to final ending*

Final ending

out the a- ges long.

Heave-HO Me Laddies

Sea Chantey

Oh if I were a sail-or out a sail-ing on the sea,___ I real-ly am quite cer-tain___ a cap-tain I would be.

Heave - ho me lad - dies. Fast - en down the sails.___

This lust - y wind will take us___ a - sail - ing o'er the sea. sea.

Lots o' Fish in Bonavist' Harbor

Newfoundland Folk Song

Verse

1. There's lots o' fish in Bon - a - vist' Har - bor,
2. Oh, Sal - ly went to church ev' - ry Sun - day,

Lots o' fish right in a - round here.
Not for to sing nor for_____ to hear.

Boys and girls are fish - in' to - geth - er,
But to see the fel - er from For - tune

For - ty - five from Car - bon - ear.
What was down here fish - in' last year.

Refrain

Oh, catch - a - hold this one, catch - a - hold that one,
Dance a - round this one, dance a - round that one,

1.

Swing a - round this one, swing a - round she;

2.

Did - dle dum dee dum, did - dle dum dee.

Over the Sea to Skye

Music by Annie MacLeod
Words by Sir Harold Boulton

Refrain

"Speed, bon - nie boat, like a bird on the wing:
"Car - ry the lad that's born to be king

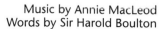

On - ward! the sail - ors cry! Skye!"
O - ver the sea to

Verse

1. Loud the winds howl, loud the waves roar,
2. Tho the waves leap, soft shall ye sleep,
3. Man - y's the lad fought on that day,
4. Burned are our homes, ex - ile and death

Thun - der clouds rend the air; Baf - fled our foes,
O - cean's a roy - al bed; Rocked in the deep,
Well the clay more could wield, When the night came,
Scat - ter the loy - al men; Yet ere the sword

*Last time, go back to
the beginning and sing to the end
(Da Capo al Fine)*

stand on the shore, Fol - low they will not dare.
flo - ra will keep Watch by your wea - ry head.
si - lent - ly lay Dead on Cul - lo - den's field.
cool in the sheath, Char - lie will come a - gain.

A Tragic Story

Music by Benjamin Britten
Words by William M. Thackeray

Start slowly **p** 1. There liv'd a sage in days of yore, And
p 2. He mus'd up - on this cu - rious case, And
More movement **mf** 3. Says he, "The mys - ter - y I've found, I'll
Getting faster **f** 4. Then 'round and 'round, and out and in, All
Faster & louder 5. And right and left, and 'round a - bout, And

he a hand - some pig - tail wore, But won - der'd much and
swore he'd change the pig - tail's place, And have it hang - ing
turn me 'round," He turn'd him 'round, He turn'd him 'round, he
day the puz - zled sage did spin; In vain it mat - ter'd
up and down, and in and out, he turn'd, But still the

sor - row'd more, Be - cause it hung be - hind him.
at his face, Not dan - gling there be - hind him.
turn'd him 'round, But still it hung be - hind him.
not a pin, The pig - tail hung be - hind him.
pig - tail stout hung stead - i - ly be - hind him.

ff

Very fast 6. And though his ef - forts nev - er slack, And though he twist, and

f slow

twirl, and tack, A - las! still faith - ful

f resolutely

to his back, The pig - tail hangs be - hind him.

Nila, Nila
MOON, MOON

Tamil Folk Song from India
Collected by Gloria Kiester

Tamil: நி - லா நி - லா ஓ - டி - வா நில் - லா - மல் ஓ - டி - வா
Pronunciation: ni la ni la o di va ni la mal o di va
English: **Love - ly, love - ly moon I see, Come down and live with me,**

மலை மேலே ஏ - றி - வா ம - ல்லி - கை - பூ கொ - ண்டு வா
ma le mæ le a ɾi va ma li gai pu kɔn du va
Slide the moun - tain to the seas, Bring me jas - mine flow - ers please.

நி - லா நி - லா ஓ - டி - வா நில் - லா - மல் ஓ - டி - வா
ni la ni la o di va ni la mal o di va
Love - ly, love - ly moon I see, Come down and live with me.

Coda

நி - லா நி - லா ஓ - டி - வா
ni la ni la o di va
Love - ly, love - ly moon I see.

Artsa Alinu
Our Land

Israeli Dance Song
English Version by MMH

Dm

Hebrew: אַר - צָה עָ - לִי - נוּ, אַר - צָה עָ - לִי - נוּ,
Pronunciation: aɾ tsa a li nu aɾ tsa a li nu
English: **Ar - tsa a - li - nu, Ar - tsa a - li - nu.**

Dm   **Am**   **Dm**   End (Fine)

אַר - צָה עָ - לִי - נוּ.
aɾ tsa a li nu
Ar - tsa a - li - nu._____

Dm   **Am**   **Dm**

כְּ - בָר חָ - רַשׁ - נוּ וְ - גַם זָ - רַעְ - נוּ,
kəvaɾ xa ɾash nu vɛ gam za ɾa nu
To our land, we come to our land._____

Go back to the beginning and sing to the end (Da Capo al Fine)

Gm   **Dm**

אֲ - בָל עוֹד לֹא קָ - צַרְ - נוּ.
a val od lo ka tsaɾ nu
Here we have plowed and plant - ed.

344

Sourwood Mountain

Appalachian Folk Song

1. Chick - en crow - in' on Sour - wood Moun - tain,
2. My true love's a blue - eyed dai - sy,

Hey de - ing dang did - dle al - ly day. { So man - y pret - ty girls / If I don't get her

I can't count them, } Hey de - ing dang did - dle al - ly day.
I'll go cra - zy,

My true love she lives in Letch - er, } Hey de - ing dang
My true love lives in the hol - low,

did - dle al - ly day. { She won't come and I won't fetch her,
She won't come and I won't fol - low,

Hey de - ing dang did - dle al - ly day.

JOHN KANAKA

American Sea Chantey

Verse

1. I heard, I heard the Old Man say,
2. We'll work to-mor-rer, but no work to-day,
3. We're bound a-way for 'Fris-co Bay,
4. A Yan-kee ship wid a Yan-kee crew,
5. Oh, haul a-way, oh, haul a-way!

John Ka-na-ka, na-ka, Tu-lai-ay!

To-day, to-day is a hol-i-day,_____
We'll work to-mor-rer, but no work to-day,_____
We're bound a-way at the break of day,_____
Oh, we're the buck-os fer to push 'er through._____
Oh, haul a-way, an'_____ make your pay._____

John Ka-na-ka, na-ka, Tu-lai-ay.

Refrain

Tu-lai-ay, Oh! tu-lai-ay,

John Ka-na-ka, na-ka, Tu-lai-ay.

HAMBONE

African American Hand Jive Game

1. Ham - bone, Ham - bone, have you heard?___
2. If that mock - in' - bird don't sing,___
3. If that dia - mond ring turns brass,___
4. If that look - ing glass gets broke,___
5. Ham - bone, Ham - bone, where you been?___

Pop - pa's gon - na buy me a mock - in' - bird.___
Pop - pa's gon - na buy me a dia - mond ring.___
Pop - pa's gon - na buy me a look - ing glass.___
Pop - pa's gon - na buy me a bil - ly goat.___
"Round___ the___ world and___ back a - gain."___

6. Hambone, Hambone, where's your wife?
   "She's in the kitchen eatin' rice."

To Stop the Train

English Round

To stop the train in cas-es of e-mer-gen-cy; Pull on the chain!___

Pull on the chain!___ Pen - al - ty for im - prop - er use, five pounds.

Waltzing with Bears

Words and Music by Dale Marxen

Refrain

He goes wa-wa-wa-wa-wa, waltz-ing with bears,

Rag-gy bears, bag-gy bears, shag-gy bears, too. There's

noth-ing on earth Un-cle Wal-ter won't do,_____ So

he can go waltz-ing, wa-wa-wa-waltz-ing, So he can go

waltz-ing, waltz-ing with bears._____

Verse

1. I went to his room in the mid-dle of the night, I
2. We bought Un-cle Wal-ter a___ new___ coat to wear, But

tip-toed in-side and turned on the light, But
when he comes home it's all cov-ered with hair, And

Last time go to Coda

to my dis - may he was no - where in sight! _____
late - ly I've no-ticed there are sev - 'ral new tears, _____

Go to the beginning (Da Capo)

— My un - cle Wal - ter goes waltz-ing at night.
— My un - cle Wal - ter goes waltz-ing with bears.

Coda

— Well, it all feels like fly - ing, there— is no de -

Go to the beginning and sing to the end (Da Capo al Fine)

ny- ing, And— now my pa - ja - mas are cov- ered with hair!

3. We told Uncle Walter that he should be good.
And do all the things we say that he should,
But I know he'd rather be off in the wood,
We're afraid we will lose him, we'll lose him for good.
Refrain

4. We said, "Uncle Walter, oh, please won't you stay,"
And managed to keep him at home for a day,
But the bears all barged in and they took him away,
For the pandas demand at least one waltz a day!
Refrain

5. Last night when the moon rose we crept down the stairs,
He took me to dance where the bears have their lairs,
We danced in a bear hug with nary a care, *(to Coda)*

Sweet Betsy from Pike

American Folk Song
Adapted by Merrill Staton

Verse

D   A7   D

1. Oh,   do   you   re - mem - ber sweet Bet - sy from   Pike,
2. 'Twas   ear - ly   one eve - ning they camped on   the   Platte,
3. They   soon reached the des - ert where Bet - sy gave   out,
4. Said   Ike, "Ole Pike Coun - ty, I'll   go   back to   you."
5. They   camped on   the prai - rie for weeks up - on   weeks.

D   E7   A7

Who   crossed the   wide   prai - ries   with   her broth - er   Ike?
By the   side   of   the   road   on   a   green shad - y   flat.
And   down   in   the   sand   she   lay   roll - in'   a - bout,
Said   Bet - sy, "You'll   go   by your - self   if   you   do.
They   swam the   wide   riv - ers   and   crossed the   tall   peaks.

D   F#m   G   D

With   two yoke of   ox - en,   a   big   yal - ler   dog,
Sweet   Bet - sy,   sore   foot - ed,   lay   down to   re - pose,
When   Ike   saw sweet   Bet - sy   he   said with   sur - prise,
There's   no time for   plea - sure   and   no   time   for   rest,
And   soon they were   roll - in'   in   nug - gets of   gold.

D   A7   D

A_____   tall Shang - hai   roost - er   and   one spot - ted   hog.
While_____   Ike kept the   watch o'er   his   Pike Coun - ty   rose.
"You'd_____   bet - ter get   up, you'll get   sand   in   your   eyes."
In_____   spite of our   trou - bles we'll   keep head - in'   west."
You_____   may not be - lieve it   but   that's what we're told.

350

Refrain

D — G

Hoo - dle dang, fol - de - dye - do, hoo - dle dang, fol - de - day.

A7 — D

Hoo - dle dang, fol - de - dye - do, hoo - dle dang, fol - de - day.

El charro
The Cowboy

Mexican Folk Song
English Version by MMH

F — C7

Spanish: Es - ta - ba un cha - rro sen - ta - do_____ en las
Pronunciation: es ta βaun cha ɾo sen ta ðo en las
English: A mourn - ful cow - boy was sit - ting_____ on the

C7 — F — 1. — 2.

tran - cas de un cor - ral._____ —
tɾan kas ðe un ko ɾal
rail - ing be - side a cor - ral._____ —

F — B♭ — F

Su ma - yor - do - mo le di - ce:_____ "No es-tés tris - te,
su ma yor ðo mo le ði se noes tes tris te
Then came his fore - man to tell him, "Don't be un - hap - py

C7 — F — 1. — 2.

Ni - co - las."_____ —
ni ko las
Ni - co - las."_____ —

Las mañanitas
The Morning Song

Mexican Folk Song
English Version by MMH

Spanish: És - tas son las ma - ña - ni - tas
Pronunciation: es tas son las ma nya ni tas
English: **Now** we sing *las ma - ña - ni - tas,*

que can - ta - ba el Rey Da - vid,
ke kan ta βael ɾei ða βið
as King Da - vid long a - go

a las mu - cha - chas bo - ni - tas
a las mu cha chaz βo ni tas
sang a song to greet the morn - ing,

se las can - ta - mos a - sí:
se las kan ta mos a si
to greet the sun - light's first glow.

Des - pier - ta, mi bien, des - pier - ta,
des pyeɾ ta mi βyen des pyeɾ ta
A - wak - en, dear one, a - wak - en

mi - ra que ya a - ma - ne - ció,
mi ɾa ke ya ma ne syo
and wel - come the ros - y dawn.

Ya los pa - ja - ri - tos can - tan,
ya los pa xa ri tos kan tan
Now the birds are sweet - ly sing - ing,

la lu - na ya se me tió.
la lu na ya se me tyo
the sil - ver moon - light has gone.

My Horses Ain't Hungry

Ter___ ___olk Song

1. My hors - es ain't hun - gry, They won't eat your hay,
2. I know you're my Pol - ly, I'm not going to stay,
3. With all our be - long - ings, We'll ride till we come

So I'll get on my po - ny, I'm go - ing a - way.
So__ come with me dar - ling, We'll feed on our way.
To__ a lone - ly cab - in, We'll call it our home.

Welsh Folk Song

1. Sleep, my child, and peace at - tend thee, } All through the night.
2. While the moon her watch is keep-ing,

Guard - ian an - gels God will send thee, } All through the night.
While the wea - ry world is sleep-ing,

Soft the drow-sy hours are creep-ing, Hill and vale in slum - ber steep-ing,
O'er thy spir - it gen - tly steal-ing, Vi - sion of de - light re - veal-ing,

I, my lov - ing vig - il keep-ing, } All through the night.
Breathes a pure and ho - ly feel-ing,

Descant *Sing Descant with lines 1, 2 and 4*

Sleep my child,_____ All through the night.

354

GARDEN SONG

Words and Music by David Mallett

1. Inch by inch, row by row,— Gon - na make this
2. Pull - in' weeds and pick - in' stones,— We are made of
3. Plant your rows straight and long,— Temp - er them with

gar - den grow,— All it takes is a rake and a hoe and a
dreams and bones, Feel the need to— grow my— own 'cause the
prayer and song, Moth-er Earth will— make you— strong, if you

piece of fer - tile ground.— Inch by inch,
time is close at hand.— Grain for grain,
give her love and care.— Old crow watch - ing

row by row,— Some - one bless the seeds I sow,
sun and rain,— Find my way in na - ture's chain,
hun-gri - ly— From his perch in yon - der tree.

Some - one warm them from be - low— 'til the
Tune my bod - y and my brain— to the
In my gar - den I'm as free— as that

rain comes tum - bl - ing down.
mu - sic from— the land.
feath - ered thief— up there.

Little Blue Top

Words and Music by Tony Hughes

Refrain

Round and round goes the lit-tle blue top,

Whirl-ing and turn-ing with nev-er a stop;

Dap-pled with white, dap-pled with brown,_____

The lit-tle blue top keeps a-turn-ing a-round._____

Verse

1. O, there's wild rag-ing o-ceans and proud moun-tain chains,
2. And there's red folk and white folk and yel-low folk too,
3. O, there's teach-ers and law-yers and med-i-cine men,
4. But there're some who are greed-y and some who don't care, And they're

Green, peace-ful val-leys and wide grass-y plains,
Black folk and brown folk to name just a few,
Pla-ces to go to and peo-ple who've been;
foul-ing our riv-ers and poi-s'ning our air. If

356

Fam' - lies of life that each set - ting con -tains,
Folks green with en- vy and____ oth - ers who're blue, And____
Oth - ers who stay home and tend to the shop, And they
all of the rest of us don't make them stop; They ____

Go back to the beginning
and sing to the end (Da Capo al Fine)

Dol - phins and spi - ders, and cat - tle and cranes.
part - ners for all these and ba - bies just new.
whirl____ and turn on the lit - tle blue top.
might end the life on the lit - tle blue top.

My Dame Hath a Lame, Tame Crane

Traditional English Round

My dame hath a lame, tame crane.

My dame hath a crane that is lame.

Pray, gen - tle Jane, let my dame's lame, tame

crane sing and come home a - gain.

YOU'RE
INVITED

Choral

CONCERT

LISTENING

CHORAL CONCERT

Clément Janequin Le chant des oyseaux
(about 1485-1560) (excerpt)

George Frideric Handel Hallelujah Chorus
(1685-1759) (excerpt) from *Messiah*

Traditional/Arranged by
Ralph Vaughan Williams Turtle Dove
(1872-1958) (excerpt)

P R O G R A M   N O T E S

Le chant des oyseaux
Clément Janequin

Clément Janequin wrote many songs that imitate sounds of everyday life, including Paris street noises, bird songs, battles, and hunting expeditions. Can you tell what is imitated in this song?

I magine that you're seated at a choral concert. You may have been greeted by an usher as you came in. The usher can help you find your seat and give you a program to read before the concert starts.

Choral singers combine their voices to achieve a special blended sound. Singers with the highest voices stand near each other because they sing the same part. The same is true for those with the middle and lowest voices. All watch the conductor, who helps them sing expressively together.

In the "Hallelujah Chorus," listen for times when the whole chorus sings together and when groups of singers sing different parts.

The soloist in "Turtle Dove" steps forward from the group as he begins. Does the rest of the chorus respond after the solo or sing along softly during the solo?

Listening

Some of the music listed below is very old, and some is new. Listen to these pieces. Which type of music would you like to learn more about?

Hallelujah Chorus
from *Messiah*

GEORGE FRIDERIC HANDEL
1741

Symphony No. 35 ("Haffner")
First Movement (excerpt)

WOLFGANG AMADEUS MOZART
1782

Erlkönig

FRANZ SCHUBERT
1815

Discoveries

The Shrovetide Fair
(excerpt) from *Petrushka*

IGOR STRAVINSKY
1919

The Dance at the Gym
(Mambo)
from *West Side Story*

LEONARD BERNSTEIN
1957

Island Rhythms
(excerpt)

JOAN TOWER
1985

The Cat and the Rat

Based on a
West Indian folk tale
Arranged by Randy DeLelles and Jeff Kriske

Down Jamaica Way

West Indian Folk Song
Adapted by
Randy DeLelles and Jeff Kriske

Long time a-go down Ja - mai - ca way,___
This is the sto-ry of their fun one day,___

1. Cat and the Rat they would like to play.___

2. Down by the sea in Mon - te - go Bay.___

Go back to the beginning and sing to the end

Lai, lai, lai, lai, lai, lai.___ Lai, lai, lai, lai, lai, lai.___

In Jamaica, people work hard farming their land. Sometimes at night they gather to tell stories. This is the story of the Cat and the Rat, who were once the best of friends. They lived side by side, and everything Cat did, Rat did, too.

Copy Cat

West Indian Folk Song
Adapted by
Randy DeLelles and Jeff Kriske

Ev'-ry-thing___ that the Cat would do,

his friend Rat___ he would do it too.

One day Cat___ made a bam-boo flute,

Go back to the beginning and sing to the end

next day Rat___ would play toot, toot, toot!

Go back to the beginning and play to the end

Recorder 1   Recorder 2   End   Recorder 1   Recorder 2

Each morning Cat and Rat left for work. On their way to the fields, they passed banana boat loaders returning from work. In Jamaica, banana boats are loaded at night, and the workers end their day when daylight comes.

Day - Oh

Jamaican Folk Song
Adapted by
Randy DeLelles and Jeff Kriske

A C

Day - oh,___ me say day - oh.___

C · 1. G7 · C · 2. G7 · C · *End*

Day-light come___ an'___ me wan' go home. · wan' go home.

B C

One bunch, two bunch, three bunch, four.___
Five bunch, six bunch, count some more!___

C · 1. G7 · C · 2. *Go back to the beginning and sing to the end.* G7 · C

Day-light come___ an'___ me wan' go home. · wan' go home.

One night Cat had a visitor. His old Uncle brought him
a very small drum. He explained that the drum had been
passed down from one generation to the next in the family.

Just Tap It

Words and Music by
Randy DeLelles and Jeff Kriske

There's a spe - cial way to play it; don't hit it, don't thump it. There's a

spe - cial way to play it and I'll tell you how. You must

ver - y gent - ly tap it; don't strike it, just tap it and the

sound you'll hear is sweet - er than a cat's me - ow!

Ostinato

Stamp *Pat* *Thump* *Gently*
        Chest *Clap*

Don't pound, don't hit, don't thump, just tap it!

Cat tapped it just as Uncle had said and he heard a beautiful, soothing sound. As Uncle left, he warned Cat not to let anyone else play the drum.

Cat's Drum

Music by
Randy DeLelles and Jeff Kriske

Hand Drum

Conga
(Second time only)

Basay Down

West Indian Folk Song
Arranged by
Randy DeLelles and Jeff Kriske

When Rat woke up the next morning, he saw Cat playing the drum. (Repeat "Cat's Drum.")

Rat begged to play, but Cat had to refuse. Thinking quickly, Rat said he had a bellyache and couldn't go to work. (Repeat "Basay Down.")

Once Cat left for work, Rat jumped up, tickled that he had fooled Cat. He hit, thumped, and poked the drum, but nothing happened. Then his hand slipped, and he tapped the drum gently instead. And the drum played. (Repeat "Cat's Drum.")

Out in the field, Cat heard the drum. He went home to see what was happening, but Rat saw him approach. (Repeat "Basay Down.") Rat pretended to take a nap. Cat decided he was mistaken and set out again for the fields. (Repeat "Basay Down.")

Rat again played the drum. (Repeat "Cat's Drum.") Rat didn't know that Cat had hidden behind a coconut palm, and Cat caught Rat in the act! (Repeat "Basay Down.")

Cat chased Rat and finally trapped him. Rat saw Cat's open mouth and sharp teeth. As Cat lunged forward, Rat threw the drum into Cat's mouth. Cat gulped twice and swallowed the drum.

Since that day, Cat and Rat have been enemies.
Cat now carries his special drum inside. He
chooses who may gently tap it. If you listen, you
can hear the special drum—Cat's purring! (Repeat
"Cat's Drum" and "Down Jamaica Way.")

Walk the Dog, Roger!

*Music and Words by Linda Worsley
and Marilyn Christensen
Story by James Abar*

Roger is late when he meets
some friends to shoot hoops.
His friends tell him to quit
daydreaming so he can be
on time.

HOOPS

Words and Music by Linda
Worsley and Marilyn Christensen

Em

1 Where you gon-na go? What you gon-na do?

Add parts 2-5, one at a time.

2 do Got to find a play-ground,———

3 do Bas - ket-ball,———

4 do Run - ning and pass - ing and

370

At home, Roger's mother asks him to PLEASE WALK THE DOG. Roger gets distracted when his sister Jean tells him that he can get in shape by trying her aerobics workout.

Shaping Up

Words and Music by
Linda Worsley and
Marilyn Christensen

One, two, three, four; One, two, three, four; One, two, three, four;

Here we go! 1.We're gon-na shape up, work out, learn to move, We're gon-na
(2.) move a-round, you just can't sit,— And do it

stretch out, reach up, and im-prove, We're gon-na one, two, three, four;
day by day un - til you're fit,—You've got to one, two, three, four;

1.
Soon we'll see— How fit and health-y we can be. You've got to
Got to do— The ex-er -

2.
Repeat Verse 2
cise that's best for you!
Dance Break
2. You've got to

3.
cise that's best for you! two, three, four; Good for you!
One,

Roger's mother reminds him to PLEASE WALK THE DOG. Jean's friends come by and invite her to the beach.

On the Sand, in the Sun, by the Sea

Words and Music by
Marilyn Christensen and Linda Worsley

1. Come a - long with me, _____ Come a -
2. Got a pic - nic lunch, _____ Come and
3. Got a game to play, _____ We can

long and see, _____
join the bunch, _____ } Out here to-geth - er — in
spend the day, _____

won - der - ful weath - er, _____
{ Swim and play and run, _____
What a day we've planned, _____
How we love to be, _____

— On the sand, by the sea, in the sun.
— In the sun, by the
— In the sun, on the

2. sea, on the sand.

3. sand, by the sea. _____

Roger daydreams about getting in shape by becoming an undersea explorer.

Under the Water

Words and Music by
Linda Worsley and Marilyn Christensen

1. Un - der the wa - ter, we swim with the fish and the
2. Un - der the wa - ter, you'll feel ver - y peace-ful and
3. *(dance)*

tide._____
free._____

Bright col - ored cor - al with
Is it a fan - ta - sy,

pla - ces for fish - es to hide._____
what is this world that you see?_____

It's like a fan - ta - sy
Fish - es go by and then,
It's like a fan - ta - sy

world in the flick - er - ing light,_____
turn - ing they swim out of sight,_____
world in the flick - er - ing light,_____

Un - der the wa - ter.

As Roger continues to daydream, joggers run by.

Jogging Song

Words and Music by
Marilyn Christensen
and Linda Worsley

Feel your heart pound, feel your heart pound,
Jog - gin' clothes on, jog - gin' clothes on,

Feel your heart beat, feel your heart beat, You've
Jog - gin' shoes on, jog - gin' shoes on, A

got to keep mov - ing, got to keep mov - ing,
mile and a quar - ter, mile and a quar - ter,

*Repeat first time only;
Last time to Coda*

Down the track, down the track,
Down and back, down and back.

Out here in the fresh air,

Out here, have - n't a care,

F♯m   Faug   F♯m   B

Out   here,   rain   or   shine,——   Just keep

Go back to the beginning, then to the Coda
Solo

A

go - ing,   you're do - ing   fine.——————   Now,

Coda

A   *Repeat to fade*

Feel   your heart—— pound . . .

Roger's mother asks him again to PLEASE WALK THE DOG.
She leaves to take her necklace to be repaired.

A bit later, Roger sees a new boy with the necklace. He wonders if the new boy has stolen it.
The dog chases the boy, and Roger chases the
dog. Roger realizes that he is a good runner!

When he catches the boy, he learns that
the boy hadn't stolen the necklace,
but had found it on the ground.
Roger makes a new friend
and finds out he can stay
in shape by WALKING
THE DOG.

Glossary

A

accelerando to get faster gradually, **187**

accent stress on a note or chord, **163**

accidental a flat (♭), sharp (♯), or natural sign (♮) that appears before a note and shows how the pitch should be changed, **233**

adagio slow, **187**

allegro fast, **187**

augment to change a rhythm by making it last twice as long, **236**

B

bar line (|) a line that divides notes into sets, showing the measures, **16**

bassoon a double-reed woodwind instrument that can play very low pitches, **188**

beat the pulse felt in music, **3**

C

call-and-response describes a song form in which each phrase sung by a solo leader is followed by a phrase sung by the group, **7**

canon song form with two or more voices performing the same melody but starting at different times, so that they overlap like a round, **11**

chord three or more pitches sounded together, **156**

D

chord root pitch on which a chord is built and that gives the chord its letter name, **158**

clarinet a woodwind instrument that uses a single reed, **239**

coda an ending section to a piece of music, **15**

crescendo (——) to get louder gradually, **116**

cumulative describes a song form in which more words are added each time a verse is sung, **12**

D

decrescendo (——) to get softer gradually, **116**

dotted quarter note (♩.) a note equal to one quarter note plus one eighth note, **108**

double reed two pieces of bamboo tied together, through which air is blown to produce the sound in some woodwind instruments, **188**

dynamics loudness and softness of music, **98**

E

eighth note (♪) two eighth notes (♫) equal one quarter note, **14**

eighth rest (⅞) the symbol for a silence the length of an eighth note, **191**

F

flat (♭) a symbol in the key signature or in front of a note that means the pitch should be sung or played a half step lower, **113**

form the order of phrases or sections in music, **22**

forte (*f*) loud, **116**

H

half note (♩) a symbol for a sound the length of two quarter notes, **14**

harmony two or more pitches sung or played at the same time, **113**

heavier register a quality of speaking or singing that usually gives louder, fuller, and lower sound, **10**

I

improvise to make up music while playing it, **166**

interlude a short musical connection between sections or verses of a musical piece, **73**

J

jazz a style of music, often using improvisation and syncopation, that grew from the spirituals, work songs, and blues created by African Americans, **166**

K

key signature the sharps or flats at the beginning of each staff, **113**

L

ledger line a line added above or below the staff, **19**

lighter register a quality of speaking or singing that gives quieter, generally higher sound, **10**

M

major the sound of music that has *do* for its tonal center and uses the pitches of a major scale, **185**

major scale a specific set of eight pitches from *do* to *do'*, **192**

measure the set of notes and rests between two bar lines, **16**

melody the tune; a series of pitches that moves upward, downward, or stays the same, **6**

meter signature a symbol that shows how many beats are in each measure and what kind of note equals one beat, **4**

mezzo forte (*mf*) medium loud, **116**

mezzo piano (*mp*) medium soft, **116**

minor the sound of music that has *la* for its tonal center and uses the pitches of a minor scale, **185**

minor scale a specific set of eight pitches from *la,* to *la,* **207**

moderato medium tempo, **187**

motive a short pattern used often in a piece of music, **71**

N

natural (♮) a symbol in front of a note that means the pitch should be played or sung as written, without a flat or sharp, **233**

O

oboe a double-reed woodwind instrument with a higher, sweeter sound than that of the bassoon, **188**

octave a skip of seven steps between two pitches; the distance between two pitches that have the same name, **142**

orchestra a large instrumental group, usually including four families of instruments: strings, woodwinds, brass, and percussion, **54**

ornamentation extra pitches or groups of pitches added to a melody to decorate it, **244**

ostinato a rhythmic or melodic pattern that repeats over and over, **30**

overture an instrumental piece that begins an opera or other large musical work; it often introduces the main musical ideas of the work, **71**

P

phrase a complete musical idea, **6**

piano (p) soft, **116**

pitch the highness or lowness of a sound, **6**

pitch syllable the name of a pitch, such as *do* or *mi*, **18**

presto very fast, **187**

Q

quarter note (♩) the symbol for one sound to a beat in $\frac{4}{4}$, **14**

quarter rest (𝄽) a symbol for a silence the length of a quarter note, **14**

R

reed a single piece of cane attached to the mouthpiece of some woodwind instruments, through which air is blown to produce sound, **239**

repeated notes one way a melody moves; to move by staying on the same pitch, **89**

ritardando to gradually slow down, **187**

S

sharp (♯) a symbol in the key signature or in front of a note that means the pitch should be played or sung a half step higher, **137**

sixteenth note (♪) four sixteenth notes equal one quarter note (♬♬), **58**

skip one way a melody moves; to move higher or lower by jumping over one or more pitches, **89**

spiritual a type of song created by African Americans, who combined African rhythms with melodies they created and heard in America, **144**

staff the five lines and four spaces on which musical notes are written, **19**

step one way a melody moves; to move by going to the next higher or lower pitch, **89**

syncopation happens when stressed sounds occur between the beats instead of on the beats of a rhythm pattern, **163**

T

tempo the speed of the beat, **187**

theme the main musical idea of a piece, **248**

theme and variations a musical form that has a main idea followed by changed versions of the idea, **248**

tie (⌣) a curved line that connects two notes of the same pitch and means that the sound is held for the length of both notes, **149**

tonal center the home tone or pitch around which a melody is centered, **45**

tone color the sound that is special to each instrument and voice, **12**

treble clef ( ) the symbol at the beginning of the staff that wraps around the G line, **64**

upbeat a note or notes that come before the first complete measure of music, **61**

variation a changed version of a theme or melody, **248**

vibration a motion that creates sound, **142**

vocables sung syllables that have no specific meaning, **143**

W

whole note (o) a symbol for a sound the length of four quarter notes, **236**

CLASSIFIED INDEX

HOLIDAYS, SEASONAL, PATRIOTIC

INDEX OF LITERATURE

INDEX OF LISTENING SELECTIONS

INTERVIEWS

INDEX OF SONGS AND SPEECH PIECES

Acknowledgments *continued*

Farrar, Straus & Giroux, Inc. for *Good-bye My Riley O* from SLAVE SONGS OF THE GEORGIA SEA ISLANDS by Lydia Parrish. Copyright © 1942 by Lydia Parish, copyright renewed © 1969 by Maxfield Parrish, Jr. Reprinted by permission of Farrar, Straus & Giroux, Inc.

Carl Fischer, Inc. for *Waltzing Matilda* adapted by Marie Cowan with lyrics adapted from A.B. "Banjo" Paterson. Copyright © 1936 by Allan & Co. Pty Ltd. Melbourne. Copyright © 1941 by Carl Fischer, Inc., New York. Copyright Renewed. Used by Permission. All Rights Reserved.

Follett Publishing Co. for *Voices of the World* by Stefi Samuelson, 1963 Follett Publishing Co., used by permission of Prentice-Hall.

Geordie Music Publishing Co. for *Golden Ring Around the Susan Girl.* © 1963, 1971 Jean Ritchie, Geordie Music Publishing Co. ASCAP.

Hap-Pal Music for *The Eagle* by Hap Palmer and Martha Cheney. © 1976 Hap-Pal Music.

Harcourt Brace Jovanovich, Inc. for *Hi! Ho! The Rattlin' Bog* from HI! HO! THE RATTLIN' BOG AND OTHER FOLK SONGS FOR GROUP SINGING, copyright © 1969 by John Langstaff, reprinted by permission of Harcourt Brace Jovanovich, Inc.

HarperCollins Publishers Ltd. for *Roads Go Ever Ever On* from THE HOBBIT by J.R.R. Tolkien. Published by George Allen & Unwin Ltd., an imprint of HarperCollins Publishers Ltd.

Mary C. Hearne for *Texas, Our Texas* by William J. Marsh. Copyright 1925 by W.J. Marsh. Copyright renewed 1953 by William J. Marsh. Reprint permission granted by Mary C. Hearne and Owen Edward Thomas.

Florence Parry Heide for *Rocks* by Florence Parry Heide. Copyright Florence Parry Heide.

Houghton Mifflin Co. for *Roads Go Ever Ever On* from THE HOBBIT by J.R.R. Tolkien. Copyright © 1966 by J.R.R. Tolkien. Reprinted by permission of Houghton Mifflin Co. All rights reserved.

Tony Hughes for *Little Blue Top* by Tony Hughes. © 1970 Tony Hughes. Used by permission.

Kid Sounds for THE CAT AND THE RAT. © 1987 Randy DeLelles and Jeff Kriske. West Indian Folk Tale retold and adapted by Randy DeLelles and Jeff Kriske.

Neil A. Kjos Music Co. for *La Pájara Pinta* from CANTEMOS EN ESPANOL BOOK I, © 1948, ren. 1975 Max and Beatrice Krone. Reprinted with permission 1992.

Rita Klinger for *Aquaqua del a Omar*, Israeli children's singing game, collected in Jerusalem, Israel, by Rita Klinger, 1980.

The Last Music Co. for *This Pretty Planet* by John Forster & Tom Chapin. © 1988 Limousine Music Co. & The Last Music Co. (ASCAP).

Limousine Music Co. for *This Pretty Planet* by John Forster & Tom Chapin. © 1988 Limousine Music Co. & The Last Music Co. (ASCAP).

Gina Maccoby Literary Agency for *Clickbeetle* from BUGS by Mary Ann Hoberman. Reprinted by permission of Gina Maccoby Literary Agency. Copyright © 1976 by Mary Ann Hoberman.

Margaret K. McElderry Books for *Finding a Way* by Myra Cohn Livingston. Reprinted with permission of Margaret K. McElderry Books, an imprint of Macmillan Publishing Company, from THERE WAS A PLACE AND OTHER POEMS by Myra Cohn Livingston. Copyright © 1988 by Myra Cohn Livingston. Used also by permission of Marian Reiner for the author.

McGraw-Hill Ryerson Ltd. for *The Old Carrion Crow*, a Nova Scotian folk song from TRADITIONAL SONGS FROM NOVA SCOTIA by Helen Creighton. © McGraw-Hill Ryerson Ltd.

Dale Marxen for *Waltzing with Bears* by Dale E. Marxen. © 1986 Dale Marxen.

MMB Music, Inc. for *The Cat Came Back* from THE CAT CAME BACK by Mary Goetze. © 1984 MMB Music, Inc., Saint Louis. Used by Permission. All Rights Reserved. For *Fed My Horse* from THE CAT CAME BACK by Mary Goetze. © 1984 MMB Music, Inc., Saint Louis. Used by Permission. All Rights Reserved. For *Nila, Nila* (aka *Lovely, Lovely Moon*) from SONGS OF INDIA by Gloria J. Kiester and Martha C. Riley. © 1988 MMB Music, Inc., Saint Louis. Used by Permission. All Rights Reserved. For *Mongolian Night Song* from SONGS OF CHINA by Gloria Kiester and Martha Chrisman Riley. © 1988 MMB Music, Inc., Saint Louis. Used by Permission. All Rights Reserved.

Page Mortimer for the movement instructions for *Down the Road*.

Music Sales Corporation for *Mambo* from WEST SIDE STORY by Leonard Bernstein and Stephen Sondheim. Copyright © 1957 (Renewed) by Leonard Bernstein and Stephen Sondheim. Jalni Publications, Inc., U.S. & Canadian Publisher. G. Schirmer, Inc., worldwide print publishers and Publisher for the rest of the World. International Copyright Secured. All Rights Reserved. Reprinted by Permission. For *This Is My Country*. Words by Don Raye. Music by Al Jacobs. Copyright © 1940 (Renewed). Shawnee Press, Inc. and Warock Corp. International Copyright Secured. All Rights Reserved. Used By Permission. For *Winter Fantasy* by Jill Gallina. Copyright © 1982 Shawnee Press, Inc. International Copyright Secured. All Rights Reserved. Used by Permission.

José-Luis Orozco for *En la Feria de San Juan* (aka *La Feria de Atitlán/La Pulga de San José*). © 1985 José-Luis Orozco. Music and lyrics ARCOIRIS RECORDS, P.O. Box 7428, Berkeley, CA 94707.

Oxford University Press for *Festival* by John Kitching from LET'S CELEBRATE—FESTIVAL POEMS, edited by John Foster.

Marian Reiner for *Finding a Way* by Myra Cohn Livingston. Reprinted with permission of Margaret K. McElderry Books, an imprint of Macmillan Publishing Company, from THERE WAS A PLACE

AND OTHER POEMS by Myra Cohn Livingston. Copyright © 1988 by Myra Cohn Livingston. Used also by permission of Marian Reiner for the author. For *To Meet Mr. Lincoln* from THERE IS NO RHYME FOR SILVER by Eve Merriam. Copyright © 1962 by Eve Merriam. © Renewed 1990 by Eve Merriam. Reprinted by permission of Marian Reiner.

Anthony Quinn Richardson for *I Can Be* by Anthony Q. Richardson. © 1991 by Anthony Quinn Richardson.

St. Nicholas Music, Inc. for *A Holly Jolly Christmas*, Music and Lyrics by Johnny Marks. Copyright 1962, 1964 St. Nicholas Music, Inc., New York, New York, renewed 1990, 1992. All Rights Reserved. Used by Permission.

Scholastic, Inc. for *Boogie Woogie Ghost* by Nadine M. Peglar. Reprinted from INSTRUCTOR magazine, October 1973. Copyright © 1973 by Scholastic, Inc. Reprinted by permission of Scholastic, Inc.

Shada Music Inc. for *I'd Like to Teach the World to Sing* by Bill Backer, Billy Davis, Roger Cook, and Roger Greenaway. © Shada Music Inc. Used By Permission.

Silver, Burdett & Ginn Inc. for *Michie Banjo*, English words by Margaret Marks, from MAKING MUSIC YOUR OWN © 1971 Silver Burdett Company. Used by permission. All rights reserved.

Kathy B. Sorensen for *Hoe Ana Te Vaka*; *San lun tsa*; and *Suk san wan pi mai*; collected and transcribed by Kathy Sorensen. © 1991 Kathy B. Sorensen.

Southern Music for *Texas, Our Texas* by William J. Marsh. Copyright 1925 by W.J. Marsh. Copyright renewed 1953 by William J. Marsh. Reprint permission granted by Mary C. Hearne and Owen Edward Thomas.

Stormking Music, Inc. for *Song of the World's Last Whale* by Pete Seeger. © Copyright 1970, 1994 by STORMKING MUSIC INC. All Rights Reserved. Used by Permission.

Sundance Music for *Walk the Dog, Roger!* by Linda Worsley and Marilyn Christensen. Copyright © 1990 Sundance Music.

Tempo Music, Inc. for *Things Ain't What They Used to Be* by Mercer Ellington and Ted Persons. Copyright © 1943 by Tempo Music, Inc. Copyright renewed 1969 by Tempo Music, Inc. Used by Permission. International Copyright Secured. Made in USA. All Rights Reserved.

Owen Edward Thomas for *Texas, Our Texas* by William J. Marsh. Copyright 1925 by W.J. Marsh. Copyright renewed 1953 by William J. Marsh. Reprint permission granted by Mary C. Hearne and Owen Edward Thomas.

The Touchstone Center for Children, Inc. for *Fire* by Patricia Taylor from MIRACLES: POEMS BY CHILDREN OF THE ENGLISH-SPEAKING WORLD. Edited by Richard Lewis. © The Touchstone Center, 1991.

Jerry Vogel Music Co., Inc. for *Macnamara's Band*. Unpub. American Version Copyright 1935 by Latham, Carlson & Bonham, renewed. Pub. American Version Copyright 1940 Jerry Vogel Music Co., Inc., renewed.

Warock Corporation for *This Is My Country*. Words by Don Raye. Music by Al Jacobs. Copyright © 1940 (Renewed). Shawnee Press, Inc. and Warock Corp. International Copyright Secured. All Rights Reserved. Used By Permission.

World Association of Girl Guides and Girl Scouts for *I Let Her Go, Go* from CANCIONES DE NUESTRA CABAÑA, copyright 1980 World Association of Girl Guides and Girl Scouts, reprinted by permission.

ART & PHOTO CREDITS

COVER DESIGN: Designframe Inc., NYC

COVER PHOTOGRAPHY: Jade Albert for MMSD

Cover Set Design by Mark Gagnon
Flute courtesy of The Selmer Company Inc.

ILLUSTRATION

Steven Adler, 56, 70-71, 106-107; Zita Asbaghi, 168-171; Susan Ash, 108-109; Steve Atkinson, 62-63; Jim Kagan Batelman, 102-103; Karen Bell, 220-222; Doron Ben-Ami, 74-75; Bob Bennett, 256-259; (calligrapher) Steven Bennett, 38, 66, 70, 86, 102, 107, 148-149, 268, 280, 300; Ami Blackshear, 180-181, 202-203; Karen Blessen, 262-263; Maxine Boll, 140-141; Sue Ellen Brown, 292-293; Shirley Chapman, 204-205; Judith Cheng, 238-239; Eva Vagreti Cockrille, 42-43; Sally Wern Comport, 86-87; Eulala Conner, 29, 57; Neverne Covington, 250-251; David Csiscko, 252-255; Margaret Cusack, 118-119; Dee Deloy, 4-5; Darius Detwiler, 10-11; David Diaz, 0-1; Nancy Doniger, 280-281; Janice Lee Durrand, 224-225; Allan Eitzen, 202; Nancy Freeman, 154; Brian Fujimori, 160-161; Manuel Garcia, 32-33; Jack Graber, 38-41; Griesbach & Martucci, 46-47; Jeffrey Gunion, 156-157; John Steven Gurney, 48-49; Randy Hamblin, 92-93, 282-283; Pam-ela Harrelson, 110-111; Dianne Teske Harris, 16-17; Kevin Hawkes, 20-21, 270-271, 362-369; Cary Henrie, 158-159; Oscar Hernandez, 14-15, 226-227; Catherine Huerta, 100-101; Richard Hull, 12-13; Susan Huls, 205; Ramona Jablonski, 94-95; Jakesevic and Lamut, 152-153; Shannon Jeffries, 166-167, 236-237; W.B. Johnson, 18-19, 26-27; Mark Kaplan, 162; Greg King, 186-187; Shannon Kriegshauser, 124-127; Dave Lafleur, 272-273; Barbara Lambase, 148-149, 284-285; Kathy Lengill, 178-179; Todd Leonardo, 44-45; Barry Maguire, 298; Mary Jo Mazzella, 142-143; Alan Mazzatti, 50-51; Sudi McCollum, 98-99; Francesca Moore, 174-175, 300-301; Marjorie Muns, 52-53; Sal Murdocca, 112-113; Randy Nelson, 54-55, 138; Carol Newson, 176-177; Nancy Nimoy, 208-209; William O'Donnell, 189; Erik Olsen, 240-241; Edward Parker, 182-183, 202-203, 274-275; Bob Pepper, 228-229; Donna Perrone, 358-359; Rodica Prato, 306-307; Bonnie Rasmussen, 60-61; Mike Reed, 88-89; William Rieser, 104-105; Robert Roper, 304-305; Robert Sauber, 22-25; John Schilling, 72-73; Fred Schrier, 288-289; Max Seabaugh, 78-81; Dorothea Sierra, 120-123; Michael Sours, 162-163; Randy South, 206-207, 248-249; Ken Spengler, 28-29; Gerardo Suzan, 66-67; Susan Swan, 184-185, 190-193; Glen Tarnowski, 194-195; Joseph Taylor, 116-117, 199; Kat Thacker, 30-31; Mary Thelen, 210-213; Gary Torrisi, 144-145; Elizabeth Traynor, 90-91; John Turrano, 34-35, 37; Jenny Vainisi, 82-85, 196-197, 266-267; Randy Verougstraete, 6-7; Carolyn Vibbert, 200-201; Pam Wall, 278-279; Mei Wang, 8-9; David Watts, 128-129, 130-131; David Wehrstein, 268-269; David Wenzel, 68-69; Kris Wiltse, 134-135; Gary Yealdhall, 230-231; Heidi Younger, 370-379.

Tech Art by TCA Graphics, Inc.

PHOTOGRAPHY

All photographs are by the Macmillan/McGraw-Hill School Division (MMSD) except as noted below.

i: instruments, Jim Powell Studio for MMSD. iv-v: instruments, Jim Powell Studio for MMSD. vi: t.l. instruments, Jim Powell Studio for MMSD. **Unit 1** 2: l. Photofest; t.r. Darryl Pitt/Retna Ltd.; m.r. Photoreporters; b.r. Frank Driggs. 3: r. Everett/Starfile. 8: Superstock. 10: Jeff Sealik/Outline. 16: The Phillips Collection, Washington, D.C. 20: Martin Fox for MMSD. 23: UPI/Bettmann Newsphotos. 26-27: FPG. 31: Ken Karp for MMSD. 32: Gordon Photographic Ltd. 41: t. Courtesy of Eva Legene; b. Kit Weiss. **Unit 2** 54-55: Jim Powell Studio for MMSD. 56: Archive Photos. 66, 67: Ken Karp for MMSD. 71: Ron Scherl/Bettmann Newsphotos. 76: Jack Vartoogian. 76-77: Dallas & John Heaton/Westlight. 77: r. Shanghai Museum. 82-83: Ken Karp for MMSD. 83: r. Motion Picture and Television Photo Archive. 85: De Croce Studio. **Unit 3** 96: t. Culver Pictures. 96-97: b. Karen Meyers for MMSD; bkgnd. Ken Karp for MMSD. 100: Mark A. Philbrick for MMSD. 103: David Heald © The Solomon R. Guggenheim Foundation, NY./Canal, 1963, Helen Frankenthaler. Purchased with the aid of funds from the National Endowment for the Arts, Washington, D.C.; matching gift, Evelyn Sharp, 1976. 104: Ken Karp for MMSD. 105: Anne Nielsen for MMSD. 106: The Granger Collection. 107: The New York Public Library. 109: Ken Karp for MMSD. 110: A.R. Linden/U.S. Marine Band. 111: UPI/Bettmann Newsphotos. 114: David Lavender. 114-115: Wesley Bocxe/Photo Researchers, Inc.; bkgnd. Ken Karp for MMSD. 118: Michael Yamashita/Westlight. 119: Marka/International Stock. 121: *Baile en Tehuankpec* by Diego Rivera, Los Angeles County Museum of Art. Gift of Mr. & Mrs. Milton W. Lipper, from the Milton W. Lipper Estate. 122-123: Ken Karp for MMSD. 124, 125: Bill Waltzer for MMSD. 128: b. Anna Lee Walter/courtesy Chronicle Books; m. Jim Powell Studio for MMSD. 129: Mark A. Philbrick for MMSD. **Unit 4** 132-133: Bill Waltzer for MMSD. 136-137: Bill Waltzer for MMSD. 138: t. Brissand-Figaro/Gamma Liaison; m.l. Faria Castro Haraldo/Gamma Liaison; m.r. Olivier Pighetti/Gamma Liaison; b. Krzystof Wojcik/Gamma Liaison. 139: l. Brissand-Figaro/Gamma Liaison; r. Peter Frey/Image Bank. 145: Iraq Musuem. 146: t. Jack Vartoogian; b. Tim Bauer/Retna Ltd. 147: t.l. Mertan Simpson Gallery; b.l. Collection of Virgil Young; LP Music Group. 150: Bill Waltzer for MMSD. 151: Caroline Davies/Liaison International; inset Caroline Davies/Liaison International. 153: Maerten van Heemskerck, *Anna Codde;* Rijksmuseum, Amsterdam. 155: Gordon Parks/Life Magazine/© Time Inc. 160-161: Bruce Caines for MMSD. 162: Paul Natkin/Outline. 164: inset David G. Hauser; bkgnd. Bill Waltzer for MMSD. 165: Joe Viesti. 169: Bill Waltzer for MMSD. 170: FPG; m.r. Photoworld/FPG. 171: r. FPG; b.r. Ken Karp for MMSD. 172: Frank Driggs/Archive Photos. 173: The Bettmann Archive. 174: r. UPI/Bettmann Newsphotos; l. Dan J. McCoy/Black Star. 175: San Francisco Craft & Folk Art Museum. **Unit 5** 185: Derek Smith for MMSD. 186, 187: Bill Waltzer for MMSD. 188: b. Harry Heleotis. 192: Bill Waltzer for MMSD. 193, 194: Bill Waltzer for MMSD. 195: Jim Stratford for MMSD. 198: Archive Photos. 200: *Down by the Riverside* by Daniel Pressley, 1966/DMA Photographers, Schomberg Center for Research in Black Culture, Art & Artifacts Division, NYPL, Astor, Lenox, & Tilden Foundation. 204: *Boy Playing Flute* by Judith Leyster, Statens Kontsmuseer, Stockholm, Sweden. 215: Marcia Keegan/Stock Market; Royal-Athena Galleries. **Unit 6** 218-219: b. Lois Ellen Frank/Westlight; Kevin Kolcyznski for MMSD. 222: t.l. NASA/Peter Arnold. 223: t.l. NASA/Peter Arnold; t.r. NASA. 231: Jim Powell Studio for MMSD. 232: Jack Kenner for MMSD. 234: American Museum, Bath, England/Superstock. 238: Mayna Treanor Avent, *Off Franklin*/Tennessee State Museum. 239: Ken Karp for MMSD. 240, 241: Bill Waltzer for MMSD. 243: © 1993 The Estate of Keith Haring. 244: m. Owen Franken/Stock Boston; b. Ken Karp for MMSD; t. Murray Alcosser/Image Bank. 244-245: m. David Frazier/Stock Market. 245: t. Frank Siteman/Stock Boston; r., m. Lynton Gardiner; b. Ken Karp for MMSD. 246: l. George Ancona/International Stock; r. Robert Frerck/Odyssey Productions. 247: b. Roland & Sabrina Michaud/Woodfin Camp & Associates, Inc.; t. Owen Seumptewa for MMSD. 252, 253, 255: Bill Waltzer for MMSD. 256: l. Granger Collection. 256-257: r. Americana Stock/Archive Photos. 258: H. Armstrong Roberts. 259: Bob Daemmrich/Stock Boston. **Celebrations** 260: Ken Regan/Camera 5. 264: t. S. Dooley/Liaison International. 264-265: bkgnd. Bill Waltzer for MMSD. 265: t.l. Linda Waidhofer/Liaison International; t.r. Jack Stein Grove/Liaison International. 276: t. Hot Shots; b. Luc A. Couturier/Départ. 286-287: Ken Karp for MMSD. 290-291: Nancy Palubniak. 294: l. David A. Harvey/Woodfin Camp & Associates, Inc.; r. Richard Shiell/Earth Scenes. 301: Roberta Barnes/Gamma-Liaison. 302-303: Steve Gottlieb Photography. 303: inset The Bettmann Archive. 306: Murauchi Art Museum, Tokyo. **Music Library** 358-359: t. Karen Meyers for MMSD; b. Superstock. 360: t.l. Angelo Hornak Photograph Library, London; t.r. Dresden/Meissen Antique Import Corporation; b. Yamaha Corporation of America. 361: t.l. MMB Music; b.l. © 1985 Steve J. Sherman; r. The Ballet Shop, New York/A. Royzman. 380: t. The Bettmann Archive; m. Herb Snitzer Photography; b. Ken Karp for MMSD.

Macmillan/McGraw-Hill School Division thanks The Selmer Company, Inc., and its Ludwig/Musser Industries and Glaesel String Instrument Company subsidiaries for providing all instruments used in MMSD photographs in this music textbook series, with exceptions as follows. MMSD thanks Yamaha Corporation of America for French horn, euphonium, acoustic and electric guitars, soprano, alto, and bass recorders, piano, and vibraphone; MMB Music Inc., St. Louis, MO, for Studio 49 instruments; Rhythm Band Instruments, Fort Worth, TX, for resonator bells; Courtly Instruments, NY, for soprano and tenor recorder; Elderly Instruments, Lansing, MI, for autoharp, dulcimer, hammered dulcimer, mandolin, Celtic harp, whistles, and Andean flute.

PRONUNCIATION KEY

Simplified International Phonetic Alphabet

VOWELS

ɑ	f**a**ther		æ	c**a**t
e	**a**pe		ɛ	p**e**t
i	b**ee**		ɪ	**i**t
o	**o**bey		ɔ	p**aw**
u	m**oo**n		ʊ	p**u**t
ʌ	**u**p		ə	**a**go

SPECIAL SOUNDS

β say *b* without touching lips together; *Spanish* nue**v**e, ha**b**a

ç **h**ue; *German* i**ch**

ð **th**e, *Spanish* to**d**o

n̩ sound **n** as individual syllable

ö form [o] with lips and say [e]; *French* ad**ieu**, *German* sch**ö**n

œ form [ɔ] with lips and say [ɛ]; *French* c**oeu**r, *German* pl**ö**tzlich

ɾ flipped r; bu**tt**er

r̄ rolled r; *Spanish* pe**rr**o

ǂ click tongue on the ridge behind teeth; *Zulu* ng**c**wele

ü form [u] with lips and say [i]; *French* t**u**, *German* gr**ü**n

ʊ̈ form [ʊ] with lips and say [ɪ]

x blow strong current of air with back of tongue up; *German* Ba**ch**, *Hebrew* **H**anukkah, *Spanish* ba**j**o

ʒ plea**s**ure

' glottal stop, as in the exclamation "uh oh!" [ˈʌ ʾo]

~ nasalized vowel, such as French b**on** [bõ]

˥ end consonants *k*, *p*, and *t* without puff of air, such as s**k**y (no puff of air after *k*), as opposed to *kite* (puff of air after *k*)

OTHER CONSONANTS PRONOUNCED SIMILAR TO ENGLISH

ch	**ch**eese		ny	o**ni**on, *Spanish* ni**ñ**o
g	**g**o		sh	**sh**ine
ng	si**ng**		ts	boa**ts**